"The battl[...]
chisel tha[...] scul[...]

A WEDDING DRESS
WITH COMBAT BOOTS

Bless you

Lily Isaacs

First printing: November 2020
Second printing: September 2021

ISBN: 978-0-578-80366-1

Written by Lily Isaacs and Shawn Smucker
Cover Design by Shawnel Corey
Cover Image by John Whitworth

With special thanks to Tim Dudley.

INTRODUCTION

The first moment I walked into Yad Vashem, the World Holocaust Remembrance Center in Jerusalem, a heavy curtain of grief threatened to smother me.

It all felt so personal.

I thought of my father in the concentration camp, when a guard struck him on the head with a brick and nearly killed him. I thought of my mother, how her friend pulled her out of a line of Jews destined for the gas chamber. The unimaginable things that my parents and their families went through hurt me to my core. I thought of all of the relatives I never met: cousins and aunts and uncles. And I thought of all the relatives I would never have because those who died would not have families of their own, nieces and nephews who never came into existence because of the ovens of Dachau or the gas chambers of Treblinka. I lost my mother's mother and two of my mother's siblings. My father lost his parents and five siblings, all killed in the Holocaust, surviving with only his half-brother.

I felt like the Holocaust robbed me of a life I would never know, stealing away people I could never meet.

It was during one of our earliest trips to Israel as a family that we first visited Yad Vashem. It was in some ways like the Holocaust Museum in Washington D.C., only much larger and more extensive, covering acres of land with multiple buildings dedicated to exhibits that memorialized the Holocaust's victims. There were an endless number of restored photographs and movies, gathered by the British and American forces when they first entered the concentration camps and ghettos spread throughout Europe. In some cases, they were the first to realize the horror of what had been going on. There had been no pictures spread through social media during the war, no satellite images taken from space. There were only these soldiers, young men, stumbling into what must have looked like hell.

It's sobering to think this kind of evil could exist in the world. I don't understand it. I can't comprehend the kind of hatred that says, "I am going to destroy you and your family, your old people and your children, your fathers and mothers, simply because of who you are." If I'm not careful, it can be terrifying, the thought of that kind of evil.

Walking around the property of Yad Vashem reminded us of the stark reality of the Holocaust. It was a look into what the camps were like, what the Germans had stolen from the prisoners, and the immense scope of the travesty. The first time I visited, every little item pierced me with sadness. The photographs from Warsaw and all the original artifacts collected from various concentration camps were each so precious to me, as if each were owned by a relative of mine.

There was the Children's Memorial. It was created from the hollowed-out space of an underground cavern and paid tribute to the 1.5 million children who had died during the Holocaust. The inside was dark except for candles that were burning, and there were mirrors everywhere, so that it looked like there were a million little flames, like stars in a galaxy. A monotone male voice read the name and age of every Jewish child killed during World War II. The voice went on and on, never stopping, and it was such an emotional experience. I could barely stand it, the thought of all those little ones, their lives snuffed out at such an early age. Someone's wide-eyed grandchild. Someone's soft-skinned baby.

Next came the Hall of Remembrance, a tent-like building that, once you were inside, had a bridge you could walk over. A memorial flame burned continuously in the building, next to a crypt. Under the bridge were slabs that looked like gravestones lying flat, and on these large stone slabs were the names of every extermination camp, concentration camp, transit camp, and killing site. And under those slabs were the ashes of Jews that they collected from each of these murder sites. Each camp name stood out to me because many members of my family were held at those camps. Some tortured, many killed.

Treblinka. Bergen-Belsen. Auschwitz. Buchenwald. Dachau. The list goes on and on.

And this was where it hit home, because I realized the ashes of my ancestors could very well be down there somewhere, under those slabs. Their remains, along with the memories of their lives, their stories, their history. My family was in that ground. My DNA was in that ground! The stuff that makes me who I am. I never got to meet those relatives, those aunts and uncles and grandparents and cousins, but somehow I could feel their presence there because we were part of each other. Our stories mingled together. That could never be stolen from us.

My children, grandchildren, and I spent a long time in the Hall of Remembrance, holding hands. Huddled together with the ones I love, I thought about my dead family members' fear, the numbness they must have felt in the camps, especially after seeing their loved ones die. They must have felt a lot of uncertainty, too — where were they? Why were they there? For how long? Who else was still alive? Would they receive food on that day or the next? Water? Would it ever end?

My mother lived through all of this. Sometimes she would share short snippets of what she had been through, and I remember a few conversations we had about God. The question she almost always raised was, "Where was God when we needed Him?" There was no anger in her voice. Only sadness and confusion. "Where was God when we prayed for mercy and no one came?"

In the silent Hall of Remembrance, we prayed, and it felt so intense. I felt the hands of my daughters, my son, my grandchildren, alive and well. I heard their voices catching as tears rose. And I tried to imagine what it sounded like when my grandparents prayed in the Warsaw ghetto. Or what my uncles' and aunts' voices sounded like, afraid and confused, just before they were killed. It felt like so much had been lost.

But spending time at Yad Vashem also felt healing, as if I were getting in touch with a part of me that had been lost long ago, a part I wasn't sure I would ever find again. And there it was, waiting for me to discover it.

~ ~ ~ ~ ~

As I get older, I think more about these things. I wonder about who I am. What is my identity, and where did I come from?

My parents were mostly silent about what they had gone through, especially during my growing-up years, so I didn't know many of the details. It grieves me that I didn't ask more questions, that I didn't push them to talk more about what they had experienced. I wish I could have held them close, especially in light of all they had lost. I was the daughter of two people who had suffered the most unthinkable horror, perhaps in the history of the world, and yet I never reached out to them because I was young, and I could only see what was right in front of me.

I hate that I did that, now that I'm older. I wish I would have asked more questions, and my previous silence pushes me to find out everything I can. I keep digging for more about my family because I want to know more. I want to go to Poland and visit the old ghetto in Warsaw; I want to walk through the death camp of Treblinka and physically breathe the air in the space where so many were lost. Not that my parents would know I was there, but I feel it honors their memory in some way when I take the time to try to understand and tell the world.

Some of the clues about where I came from reside in my present body and in knowing who I am, understanding my personality. For example, I know I often guard my true feelings from others. I do a good job of appearing strong and independent when actually I feel very vulnerable and often second guess myself. I'm devoted to the people I love and would do anything for them. But I also put quite a bit of work into maintaining a wall around my own heart, keeping a safe distance from anyone who might hurt me or take advantage of me in some way. I recognize my tendency to surround myself with safe people, those who I know love me. If someone hurts me or crosses me, that wall goes up around my heart.

These are just a few of the things I know about myself, and I wonder, how many of these characteristics would be found in the relatives I lost? Did I have a great-aunt who always appeared strong while crying herself to sleep at night? Did I have a cousin who was devoted to those she loved? Did I have uncles who surrounded themselves by safe people, people who they knew loved them, and were skeptical of strangers?

I keep following the clues to who I am. I keep digging deeper.

~ ~ ~ ~ ~

I think I've always struggled with discovering, and being comfortable with, my identity. As a young girl growing up in an immigrant family, I felt a sense of urgency to fit in, to do anything I had to do to make sure I was just like all the other kids in my neighborhood. This was nearly impossible, though, and I always felt my family was imperfect and even flawed—maybe because my mother was always out late with her boyfriends, or because of my alcoholic father and the way he embarrassed me in front of my friends. I never felt like I fit in, so I tried to create a new identity, one I thought my friends would like, one I wouldn't feel so uncomfortable with.

But it wasn't just my family that made me want to change my identity. I felt like I was constantly fighting against my own flaws, always trying to overcome these weaknesses and become someone better than who I was. Early in my life, there was the scoliosis that curved my spine and forced me to wear a cumbersome back brace. I always felt self-conscious and that life was unfair. After that, I tried to break out of my shyness and hesitancy. What began as an insecurity about my family turned into a deep insecurity about myself, something that I tried to navigate for many years.

As I got older, these insecurities brought about a toughness in me, a strong desire to thrive and to make my parents proud. I was determined to overcome all of those disadvantages, and I dreamed of becoming something more, someone more valuable. I became a performer, an actor, and then a singer, and the whole time I was trying to prove that I wasn't just shy little immigrant Lily with scoliosis and a different kind of family. If I worked hard enough, if I became talented enough, I could become important, maybe even famous. Once I was famous, I wouldn't have to worry about people not liking me or thinking less of me. Everyone would love me.

That last line makes me laugh. How much I have learned!

Years passed, and many of the things I thought were part of my central identity shifted. I became a Messianic believer, a wife, a mother, a cancer survivor, then a divorcee, and a grandmother. Despite many hardships, I began to feel more comfortable in my own skin. I have seen firsthand through many different experiences that I am not a quitter. I am resilient. When I was young and devoted to my family's version of Judaism, I thought I was only a dot in the universe, here one day and gone the next, but once I became a believer, I realized that God had a plan for my life. I wasn't insignificant! I wasn't worthless! And I didn't have to become famous to be loved — God loved me just as I was.

So who am I?

I am recognizing now that my identity is made up of many different aspects, many different hats, many different roles. We're all that way—we all have multiple responsibilities, gifts, and things to do in our lives. We can be children, grandchildren, parents, or grandparents. We can be employees or employers. We can be survivors or warriors or spouses. We can be imperfect, codependent, addicted, and abused. There are so many identities, some chosen and others thrust upon us. There are things we strive for, and there are things we inherit.

But above and beyond all of these different identities, I have a primary identity, and it lies at the heart of who I am. Sometimes we need our friends to remind us of who we are.

This happened for me during a prayer meeting when I was going through one of the most difficult times of my life. I'll tell you more about the details later in the book, but for now you should know what my friend, a pastor, told me while he was praying over me.

"Lily, I have to tell you this. While we prayed over you, I saw a vision and you were standing there wearing a wedding dress with combat boots on."

That picture stayed in my mind for a long time. It still does today. It's a funny thought yet so sobering.

I am the bride of Christ. I am wearing a wedding dress, bathed in love and adoration, cared for in such tender ways. But I am also wearing combat boots, because life is hard, and I know, after many struggles, that sometimes I just have to keep putting one foot in front of the other.

I have stared down so many monsters. I have fought so many battles. I have weathered so many storms.

Thinking back through it all, I recently had a revelation. Many times in my life, during hard times or unexpected tragedy, I felt like I was standing on the edge of a cliff. With my arms raised up to heaven and my mind in turmoil, these situations left me feeling so lonely, so desperate, and one step away from destruction. There was my cancer diagnosis. There was the long period of time where my brother and I had to care for our aging mother. Loneliness. Depression. Anxiety. Fear. A struggling marriage. I felt all of these things, and so often it felt like they were taking me to the edge.

But somehow, during every hardship, the Lord reached out and held me, kept me from falling. And in those moments, I was reminded of my many identities, my many experiences, and the many ways that I live in this world.

I am a daughter.

I am a mother.

I am a divorcee.

I am a warrior.

I am a singer.

I am a peacemaker.

I am an encourager.

I am private.

I am transparent.

I am angry.

I am happy.

I am a friend.

I am a survivor.

I am a grandmother.

I am a child of God.

I am an author.

I am a mosaic, made up of so many facets, so many surfaces. I have jagged edges, but they all fit together. And I still have stories to tell.

As I share my heart and my life experiences with you, I pray you can come with me through my joys, my heartaches, my battles, and my victories. I will never understand how I got through all of it, but God has kept me. He never let me fall. I hope my experiences will help you see through your current difficulties in a new way and give you hope. I hope these stories will help you remember that God is with you, and that your true identity, more than any of these other titles, is the beloved of Christ.

That is the only identity that matters.

CHAPTER
1

It was a warm October day in Texas in 1998 when I got the phone call. We were scheduled to perform that night, but Joe wasn't traveling with us that weekend. In fact, it had been quite a few months since he had traveled with us. The day felt like just any other day when we're on the road — we had left the bus and were getting ready to go out and have some lunch. After that, Ben and our staff would work on the sound equipment and we'd do a sound check, finish preparing for the concert, and relax for a minute before the show began.

But as I walked out of the bus, my phone rang, so I answered it.

"Mrs. Isaacs?" a voice asked, and although the voice was familiar, at first I wasn't sure who it was.

"Yes?" I asked. The man said his name, which I recognized. My divorce lawyer. My heart sank and I stopped walking.

"Well," he said in a quiet voice. "Mrs. Isaacs, I have to tell you that your divorce is final today. I am sorry for all of the trouble."

"Thank you," I whispered, not knowing what else to say. He said a few more things, but I couldn't pay attention because my mind was racing. I didn't know how I should feel. Happy? Sad? Relieved? Depressed? While I was thinking all of these things, he finished talking. It was quiet for a moment.

"Mrs. Isaacs?" he asked. "Are you still there?"

"Yes, I'm sorry. Thank you."

We said goodbye, and I stood there for an extra moment, frozen in time, still holding the phone up to my ear, even though there was no one on the line any longer.

That was it. A simple phone call served as the announcement. I turned around and went back into the bus. I wasn't hungry anymore. After 28 years, my marriage was over.

~ ~ ~ ~ ~

If you read my first book, *You Don't Cry Out Loud,* then you know a lot about the early musical journey our family was on, from playing in front of small churches in the 1970s and '80s to performing for huge audiences in the '90s. The children progressed musically in ways I never could have imagined. They had natural talent coupled with a desire to learn and improve. Combined, these turned them into accomplished musicians at young ages.

We moved to Tennessee in 1991, all the way from Ohio, to a beautiful property and home that felt like a dream come true. It was the first big house we had ever lived in. The kids could each have their own bedroom, there was a living room and a family room, and there were a few acres outside where we could get out and stretch our legs. It was such an exciting time.

We seemed to settle in quickly. I mean, there are always bumps when you make a move, especially with teenagers, but it went as smoothly as it could have gone. Sonya and Ben were in college, and Becky, who had been hesitant to make the move, was a senior in high school. But the move did take her closer to her serious boyfriend at the time, John (whom she later married), so it wasn't too hard to convince her that moving to East Tennessee was a good idea.

We had chosen the area because we had close friends there, people we often stopped to see when we were on the road. It was also a lot closer to the part of Kentucky where Joe's family lived, and he started spending more time up there, sometimes packing a bag and leaving Monday, returning in time to hit the road with us on Thursday. I was okay with that. I was glad he could see his family, and we were all so busy anyway. We barely saw each other when he was at home.

There were hard things going on during those years, but we had some really good times too. There was no feeling like walking out on stage in front of an excited crowd that buzzed with anticipation. Joe and I were proud of the children, and we all sang and testified to what God was doing in our lives. The kids were wonderful. We ministered from our hearts, and people came to the altar, weeping, praying, and seeking God. Those were good nights. Later, at the merchandise table, people complimented us on how good we sounded and how impressed they were with the children. They'd talk about how one of Joe's recent songs touched their lives, or how they had shared it with a friend in need. Sometimes we'd even get to go out to eat with old friends after the show and catch up. We all laughed and had a great time. Life seemed normal and good. For a long time.

But below the surface, things were getting worse. Joe and I fought more. He was gone more. Tension made its way onto the stage. It got really, really hard.

~ ~ ~ ~ ~

Even if you have a wonderful family and your life is full of good friends, you will at some point find yourself feeling very alone. Maybe it's some kind of failure you didn't see coming, or a time of financial difficulty. Maybe it's depression or maybe it comes after you lose someone you love. Maybe it's a tough diagnosis. These can be some of the hardest times of life, when we find ourselves walking our life's journey feeling unexpectedly alone.

This is where I found myself in the mid-'90s.

My marriage was falling apart.

Divorce is such a strange thing. Growing up the way I did, divorce felt like just about the biggest failure I could endure. I knew very few people who were divorced, and in my mind, I was going to do whatever I had to do to keep my marriage together. But a marriage is made up of two people, and both have to be dedicated to its health. One person, on their own, can't make a successful marriage.

Joe and I had experienced a lot of problems as newlyweds — we were both barely twenty, we were both very immature, and I think a lot of my expectations for marriage were unrealistic. I had created a fairy tale in my mind based on movies or things I saw on television. But Joe and I were different in so many ways. Our outlooks on life couldn't have been any further apart, simply because of our upbringing. Joe was a country boy raised by conservative Christians, and I was a city girl who had grown up in a Jewish family.

Both of us came into the relationship with baggage, but in spite of everything, our marriage lasted for 28 years. Nearly three decades. That's a lot of time to spend with one person, a lot of years to invest in a relationship that you suddenly realize isn't going to survive. There came a point when we couldn't make it work any longer, no matter how badly anyone wanted it to.

As our relationship crumbled in the '90s, before our divorce was final, Joe moved out and returned to where he grew up in Kentucky. The kids and I did our best to move on without him. At first, I have to admit, I was terrified. How could The Isaacs be a band without Joe Isaacs? But his exit from our group had been coming for a long time. He suffered a back injury in 1981, had several back surgeries, and continued to suffer with back pain. He had missed quite a few dates here and there for a few years, so in some ways we had gotten used to performing without him. And I had always taken care of the accounting side of things, so that wasn't an added stress. Once he had officially moved on, we really had to embrace what we had left: me and the three kids.

Of course, the children were grown by then and knew that Joe and I had been experiencing problems in our relationship. They saw everything that was going on. They could see the pain I was in. But very few people besides my children knew what I was going through: the heartache, the sense of failure, the determination to keep my life going. I'm a very private person, for better or for worse, and I don't expose my life on social media or talk about my personal life onstage unless it's part of a testimony to praise the Lord. I have a very small circle of friends who I sometimes talk to and ask for prayer, but besides that, very few people know what's going on in my life.

This is why, for a long time, when people would ask us where Joe was, we simply said he wasn't feeling well — even after we were separated. And it was true, his back was bothering him a lot, and he would have been missing a lot of those dates anyway, even if our marriage had been good.

Sonya did a lot of the emcee work, and Ben stepped in to run the logistics side of things: setting up equipment, taking care of the bus, etc. Becky led some songs, and I was doing my best to keep everything on track when it came to dates and scheduling. I felt like I was always on the phone, always taking calls and arranging concerts, sometimes trying to shoehorn in another appearance or switch dates when something didn't work out.

~ ~ ~ ~ ~

A few months after our divorce was final in 1998, Joe called me and said he wanted me to tell people about the divorce. People were seeing us in separate places and beginning to wonder what was going on. I agreed, and I went on our website and put an update there, saying that, unfortunately, as life sometimes goes, Joe and I were divorced. We continued to be friends. That's about all I wrote, keeping it short and to the point.

Again, I was terrified. What would people say? How would they respond? Would churches stop booking us because of the divorce? Would our friends leave me? I had tried so hard to stay married because we were in ministry. I was embarrassed for people to find out what it was actually like in our home. We had reached so many people with our singing, giving them encouragement and hope. What if people who we encouraged doubted the message we had carried to them once they saw how broken our family was?

Could I tell everyone about my failure? How could God ever make anything good come out of this?

And again, my worries proved groundless. Our fans accepted us with open arms, and more and more people came up to me after each concert, wanting to share their own struggles.

Eventually I had to tell my mother and stepfather that Joe and I were divorcing, which I wasn't eager to do. They never knew much about my singing career or really understood it. Of course, they knew my children were adults and that we were singing together, but they never really asked about the details. They were never interested in talking about Christianity, and the few times we did before my father died, he would get frustrated and upset.

But eventually I told Mother about my failing marriage. I eased her into it, first telling her we were having trouble and then later telling her about the divorce. I didn't know what she would think or say, but she was always an advocate for being happy, and she was okay with it.

It was the same on Joe's side of the family. He has a lot of siblings who I'm still close to and stay in touch with. His nephews and nieces still call me Aunt Lily, which I love. They still reach out to me and want to see the children and me. They still show me a lot of love.

You know, besides that short note I left on the website about the divorce, I've never talked publicly about why we divorced. I guess I just never thought it was anyone else's business.

A few years later, as things continued to grow and our group got even stronger, we decided to incorporate the business. This brought in a whole new dynamic. It was no longer this feeling of me and my kids. We became partners, and that has continued right up until today. When we are on the road, we are business associates. It's a different relationship that brings with it a different level of respect. We treat each other as equals now.

At home I'm still their mom. We're a normal family who talks throughout the day. I don't see them every day, but if I cook dinner, I invite them over. I pick up grandkids at school or run to the store. Daily stuff like that. Of course, we have business things that pop up throughout the week, but I never try to throw the mother card at them when it comes to business, and I want the week to be a time when I can be a mother and grandmother.

This whole process freed up the kids to move into their own style without feeling that they were being disrespectful of me, and I have to tell you that sitting back and watching it happen has been one of the great joys of my life. Their increasing independence, as individuals and as artists, is so inspiring.

Those days when Joe was part of the group were so incredibly important to forming who we would become as The Isaacs, but that's so far in the past now that it almost feels like a dream to me. When I think back on those days, I try to focus on the good times. But the pain is real too.

~ ~ ~ ~ ~

There is a particular kind of loneliness that comes when a marriage dissolves. Divorce, at the end of the day, is a road that in many ways you have to walk alone, even if you have a lot of family and friends around you. There is a numbness that sets in, a sense that nothing else really matters, that you might never recover from this.

After I divorced, I was more devastated about being alone than anything else. It was scary, not having the security of someone else in the house who knew what to do when something needed to be repaired. It was lonely going to a doctor's appointment by myself, not knowing what the diagnosis might be. When a storm would arrive in the middle of the night and the electricity went out, or when I'd think about having a medical emergency and being on my own, I felt afraid. For many years, it was hard to be by myself. After having a house full of people for most of my life, being the only person home was difficult. But I have learned how to live a different life, a single life.

And I had the advantage of a supportive family. Whenever I needed anything, my kids were there. I didn't want to be too needy, so I did a lot of things on my own, and that helped me to grow up. But I got a lot of help too. My girls were always around when I needed them, Ben called me almost every day on his way to the studio (when we weren't traveling together), and Becky's husband, John, mowed my grass and helped me around the house a lot.

You know, the other thing that happened for me after the divorce is that I started to remember who I truly was. I had been silenced for so many years, not because my marriage demanded that of me, but because of how our personalities meshed. Joe was always the life of the party, so I tended to shrink back and stay out of the spotlight. That's just how it went. You can't have two dominant people in a relationship.

But I lost myself, and soon after the divorce, I discovered who I was again. I remembered that I wasn't afraid to take chances. After all, I was the girl who acted on stage in high school and went to a theater summer camp in Woodstock, New York. I took my younger brother on the subway to our first Christmas party in Manhattan. I even went to the Woodstock Folk Festival, and to the first Beatles concert at Shea Stadium with thousands of other people. My friend Maria and I had landed a recording deal with Columbia Records when we were still teenagers. I took my first airplane flight in 1970 by myself to meet Joe's family — and I was terrified! And I had moved away from the city, following Joe on our first adventure. Somehow, through the years, I had forgotten how much I loved adventure, new things, and new places.

I was a risk-taker, and I remembered that I could drive for long distances by myself. I could even live alone. Remembering these things, and seeing them wake up in me, felt liberating. I felt strong again. And I felt free. I didn't have to fix supper if I didn't want to. I didn't have to consider anyone else when I wanted to buy something. I didn't have to include anyone else in my plans (although to this day I do have to give an account to my three grown children).

I was able to be the kid I had been in my teens, young and carefree and doing what I wanted to do. And in this, I found myself again. I found my voice and my personality.

But these revelations didn't arrive the day my divorce was final. It took me some time to learn all of these things about myself.

~ ~ ~ ~ ~

All of my kids were grown and out of the house by the time Joe and I divorced, living their own lives with their own spouses and children and dreams and concerns. I desperately wanted to stay in my home, so I remortgaged the house. Joe and I divided everything. I had a babysitter who traveled with us to help with the grandkids, and when we weren't traveling, she lived in my house. I remember one day, when the house was empty, I was carrying my laundry from the basement so that I could fold it in the living room.

There I was, nearly fifty years old, my children grown and gone, living in a 4,200-square-foot home all by myself. There were five bedrooms and three bathrooms, and they were almost all empty. When we had moved to that house, it had been my husband and me and our three rambunctious teenagers, and we had been caught up in the dream of owning such a beautiful place. But there I was, only five years later, all alone in the quiet.

The weight of sadness and loneliness became too much to bear, and I couldn't make it all the way up the stairs. It hit me like a ton of bricks. I sat on the landing in between floors, dropped the basket, and I wept. Right there, surrounded by my unfolded laundry.

Sometimes it's good to have a nice, long cry. I sat there for a few moments, and I let myself feel what I was feeling. I cried for all that I had lost, including the future I had envisioned. I no longer had any idea what it would look like.

I took a deep breath, dried my eyes, picked up the laundry, and took it up the steps. This was one of those moments when I had to put on my combat boots. I knew I had to keep going, keep fighting. If I gave in, if I let myself crumble under all of the pressure and worry and sadness, I didn't think I would ever recover. I would become a shell of myself, unable to cope with anything in life.

What I should have done, along with putting on my combat boots and getting up, was to find some good counseling. I regret not doing that. If you're in any kind of difficult situation, if you're divorced or have been abused or feel depressed, please talk to someone. Get professional help. Divorce, or the breaking up of any important relationship, is a road best not traveled alone. Because I didn't go for any kind of help, I held on to feelings much longer than I should have. I harbored unforgiveness that kept me bitter for a much longer time than was necessary.

But I kept going.

~ ~ ~ ~ ~

A few months after the divorce was final, Christmas came around. We usually celebrate at my house with my kids and grandkids, but during the first Christmas after my divorce, all of the kids were married, so we were splitting time. We picked an off-day to celebrate together, maybe the night after Christmas.

On Christmas Eve, I was by myself. The kids were all off with their spouses' families. My mother was in New York City. The babysitter who lived with me had gone home for the holidays, and I was alone in that big, empty house.

My kids kept calling and making sure I was okay, and I kept telling them, "Go! Be with your family! Have a good time!" I think I ate a cheese sandwich and watched about six hours of movies in my living room. It was a sad night, but I didn't want to tell my children about it. I didn't want to spoil their Christmas or have them worrying about me.

That was one of the loneliest nights I ever had in my life. I didn't decorate a lot for Christmas, although I think that year I did put a Christmas tree up for the kids. We had never celebrated Christmas in New York when I was growing up, so as I got older it was more about making it special for my kids. When you don't grow up with a holiday, it's not as big of a deal.

I remember standing at the dining room window on Christmas Eve, before it got dark, looking out through the blinds and into the approaching night. I felt like I was on an island in the Pacific, somewhere all by myself. My heart felt like it took up my whole chest, and a heaviness hovered over me. I wondered how I had gotten to that point. How had my life taken this strange and unexpected turn? What would the rest of my life look like?

Maybe I needed that night, you know? Maybe I needed to have a night like that to mourn all that I had lost, mourn the life I wouldn't have with a husband by my side in my later years. It was a tough welcome into the life of being divorced.

Divorce is a strange thing. Even though things hadn't been good between Joe and me for a long time, my feelings were still hurt by our separation. I felt like I wasn't good enough. I felt like I must have done something wrong, and I ruminated on that for many years, thinking back over mistakes I had made or things I might have done differently to keep it all together. I know the truth now, but it took me a long time to get here.

~ ~ ~ ~ ~

A woman came up to me after one of our concerts. She started off with small talk, questions about a few of the songs, but I could tell there was something she wanted to talk about, something deeper. She had sad eyes. Then she told me she was recently divorced.

"Are there any Bible verses that have helped you get through your dark times?" she asked me, and while the Bible is so important to me, I knew that she was looking for more than a cute saying or even a passage of scripture.

"For the first year or two, you'll probably cry a lot," I told her, and tears welled up in her eyes. She nodded, and I kept going. "You'll probably battle with feelings of inferiority. You'll wonder if you can ever be good enough, for yourself or anyone else. There will be days or weeks or months where you won't want to eat. Then, unexpectedly, you'll gain weight."

We both laughed through the tears.

"You should definitely see a counselor," I suggested.

"It's hard to go to bed by myself at night," she said. It was my turn to nod. I knew that feeling.

"You'll learn to do all kinds of new things," I said. "Change the lightbulb in the refrigerator, climb a tall ladder, file your taxes — it's time for you to put on your combat boots."

She sniffed and blew her nose. "I feel kind of, I don't know, broken? I can't put my finger on it."

"It's hard," I agreed. "It is really hard. But you will find your way. You'll get through it. There is life after divorce, and you'll get used to living alone and being alone at night. You might even grow to enjoy it. I talk to myself now. No one argues with me, and I'm always right."

She laughed through her tears.

"I do!" I insisted. "If people were in the house with me, they would think I was crazy. But God hears me too, so I always pray out loud. When I go to bed at night, I sleep with my Bible under my pillow. Do you have people nearby who can help you?"

She nodded.

"People have come into my life who will help me," I said. "And it's been so important. My son, Ben, or my sons-in-law, John and Jimmy.

I talk to my daughters every single day, and they come with me to my doctor appointments. I didn't think I'd be able to do all the normal things a life requires, but I can, sometimes by myself, and sometimes with a little help from my friends. I have done things on my own that I never thought I'd be able to do. I've driven myself to scary doctor appointments, and flown all around the world."

"Thanks, Lily," she said. "I know I'll get there. But I still feel so broken."

I hugged her. "There is a trauma that can come along with divorce that might not ever completely go away. When you have loved someone deeply, you miss them when they're gone. The pain is hard. But you can do it. Keep going."

I watched her walk away. When I was first divorced, the enemy was constantly trying to tell me things in order to influence how I thought.

Lily, you're not good enough.

Lily, you can't make it on your own.

Lily, what will you do when you get old?

Lily, how will you pay all the bills?

Lily, you can't make a living as a single person.

The only way I could silence those voices was by spending time with God, praying and reading scripture, seeking after Him. And then I heard His voice, His thoughts towards me.

Lily, you are more than enough.

Lily, you can make it, with my help.

Lily, I will always be here for you.

Lily, I will always provide for you.

Lily, I will help you.

For some, divorce might feel liberating. If you're the one filing for divorce, and you've been abused, good for you. No one should have to live a life being abused by their spouse. I admire men and women who have the inner strength to walk away from an abuser when they can't work it out through counseling. Life is too short for that.

Forgiveness is one of the most important things in life. It's such a big deal, and it can be liberating in ways I never imagined. The only way you can heal from life's big disappointments, like divorce, is if you can truly forgive. It's not something that happens overnight — trust me — you have to be willing to surrender every day, lay down the pieces of yourself that are clinging to bitterness and selfishness and fear. You have to find it in your heart to forgive.

Only then can you move on.

~ ~ ~ ~ ~

Soon after my divorce, I sat in my office on a Monday morning, working on the bank deposit from the previous week. I was exhausted. My mind was burdened by everything that was going on, and I was trying to cope with it all. Mondays are always busy. Usually we arrive home late Sunday night or early Monday morning, I have a fair amount of work to catch up on, and it all seems so quiet after being on the road with the family for a week.

It's nice, though, the peace, the stillness. I pray a lot. I think a lot.

I had picked up the mail from our post office box earlier in the morning and decided to go through it before I continued with the office work on my desk. There was a letter in the mail addressed to me, and it looked a little dirty, as if it had been misplaced or sitting somewhere, forgotten about for a long time. The return address wasn't one I recognized — maybe it was a letter from a fan.

I opened it. The letter was from a man I didn't know, and he started by telling me his story. I'll refer to him as Buddy. He was homeless, living in his old car behind a gas station near Atlanta, Georgia.

"One day," he wrote, "on my daily routine of going through the dumpsters looking for food, I found a magazine that someone had tossed. It was a *Singing News* magazine. I never pick up these types of things, but that day I just did. It had an article in it written by a Jewish lady from NYC. She grew up in New York, moved to Ohio, and received Yeshua as her Messiah at the age of 23."

He had read my story in the magazine, and it had touched him so much that he had written me a letter.

He was also from New York, and I think that's what grabbed his attention. Anyway, he went on to tell me how he was moved by my story. He didn't ask for a thing.

I prayed about it, and later that day I shared it with my family. I decided I would write him back. I thanked him for writing to me, tried to encourage him, and told him I'd be praying for him. I sent it to his name, using the gas station as the address.

Within a few weeks, I received another letter from him. This went on for a few months, and we basically just started a little friendship. The letters were always nice and cordial, and I prayed for him daily. Though he never asked for anything, I always put a $20 bill in with the letter and told him to get something hot to eat. After a few letters, I sent him a Bible, signed it from our family, and wrote in the note, "I am praying for you, Buddy, and you said that my story touched you. Here is a book I want you to read. It has not only touched me but changed my life."

I sent the package to the gas station where he was allowed to park his car, hoping he would receive it. Within a few weeks, I received a note from him thanking me for the Bible. He said he was reading it. A few months after that, he wrote to tell me that he had been sleeping in his car, where he lived, and woke up one morning to find the sun was rising. He said he looked up to the heavens and asked God into his heart. He said he felt so warm, like God had forgiven him for everything he had done wrong.

I wrote back and told him how proud I was of him. I even considered going to Georgia to try to find him. Then, one day around Christmas time, my family and I put together a package for him, including a couple of sweatshirts, socks, warm hats and gloves, and a blanket. We wrapped each item separately, just to make it special.

Within a few weeks, I heard from him again: he was so thankful for everything we had sent, and he was opening one package a day so that it would last him through the holidays. I sent him another letter and asked him if he had a way to play CDs because I wanted to send him some of our music.

But then he said something that shocked me.

"I would love to be able to listen to your CDs and hear all of you singing, but I have been deaf since birth."

I couldn't believe it. My heart just broke for him.

But I was also amazed at how God worked — I was part of a singing ministry. That's how we reach people for God. Yet this homeless man found the Lord without ever hearing us sing a note. That blew my mind.

God works in mysterious ways.

We continued writing to each other for several years, until one day we received a note that had a photo of him inside it. He had restored his relationships with his family, and he had a new granddaughter.

They named her Lily Rose.

I think he must have passed away, because I haven't heard from him in several years.

~ ~ ~ ~ ~

Going through that divorce was one of the hardest things I've ever had to do. But somehow God worked through that difficult time and connected me with so many other wonderful people.

I filed for divorce in the summer of 1998. That also just so happened to be when our band hit its first real challenge: Sonya stepped away from The Isaacs to record her first album for Lyric Street. It was an incredible opportunity for her, but we weren't sure what we would do without our lead singer. Becky was more than capable of stepping into that role, but before we knew it, she was dealing with some health challenges that would stretch all of us to our limit.

CHAPTER
2

For years, The Isaacs had been sailing along without any major challenges. Sure, Joe and I navigated a difficult marriage, and there were always the typical issues that come with raising teenagers and traveling every weekend and trying to be creative. We clashed over this song or that set list. But we had settled into a kind of normal that, for the most part, worked for our family.

Then came the divorce, and that was a monumental change. We had to adjust to the finality of that news, what it meant for me and the family and the band. We found ourselves moving into a new space relationally but also musically. We were making adjustments to our sound, and the kids were writing their own songs. Everything was new, which was both exciting and terrifying.

In the midst of all this change, another domino fell, one that added to my anxiety: Sonya was offered the opportunity to perform in country music and record with Lyric Street Records. This was something she had always dreamed of doing. She loved performing, loved singing and playing, and a move into country music would offer her even more opportunities than we had seen in the country gospel music scene.

But Sonya was our lead singer, and ever since Joe had moved on, she had been doing a lot of our emceeing. When your music group is your family, and there are four of you, each of you plays a huge role. We had a great band with us at the time — my son-in-law John (who was faithful to our ministry for over 12 years), Tim Surrett, and Jeff Tolbert, to mention just a few. They were an important part of the band, especially through that time of change, but what would we do without Sonya as our lead singer?

I didn't want to stand in the way of what might turn out to be her big break. None of us did. Becky, Ben, and I talked about it, and we knew she needed to give it a shot. I tried to be supportive and encouraging and excited for her, but on the inside, I was a ball of worry and anxiety. How would we continue to make The Isaacs work with both Joe and Sonya gone in such a short span of time? Would people start to get upset when we showed up for performances without the patriarch of the band or the person who usually sang lead?

The first thing I had to do, and it was something I dreaded, was to explain to our promoters that Sonya would not be traveling with us. It was a phone call I didn't want to make. Our shows are lined up over a year ahead, so when people scheduled us, it was under the assumption that our entire family would be there. I was nervous that some might back out of shows.

What would we do financially if we lost a lot of tour dates? Where could I find a job? I tried to imagine what I would possibly do at the age of 50, when I had very little experience outside of the music industry. What would the children do for a living? I thought of each of them and what their strengths were. All three of them had gone to college and could choose another career, but this was their calling. As is often the case, my mind raced far ahead of the current reality, trying to figure out what could go wrong so that I could fix it before it even happened.

I started making those dreaded phone calls, but when I spoke with the promoters, I emphasized that it was a temporary thing, that Sonya would be back with us soon. The rest of us would still be there, singing the same songs with the same heart and passion. And you know what? We didn't lose a single date. We managed to keep every-thing afloat, pay the bills, and keep singing.

We hired a mandolin player, Adam Steffey, to take Sonya's place, maintaining a full band, but a lot of the responsibilities for singing lead fell to Becky. At that point in her life, she was very shy and suffered from a lot of anxiety when it came to our shows. She was extremely talented, but the weight of so much additional responsibility outside of her comfort zone was almost too much.

In the middle of everything, during Sonya's absence and Joe's leaving, the audience still had no idea what we were going through. They didn't realize yet that Joe and I were split up or that I was scared for the future of The Isaacs. We just kept singing, because that's what we did when things were hard. It's what we still do, no matter what circumstances we're going through.

We sing.

After traveling for three months with Vince Gill, Sonya came back and rejoined us on the road. And in a way, everything felt like it was coming back together — just having all of my children in the bus again, and hearing them sing their parts, gave me an incredible sense of peace in the middle of what was otherwise a very trying time.

We got into a good groove.

~ ~ ~ ~ ~

Back when Becky was 17 or 18, she started having stomach prob-lems. Her digestive system was going haywire, and while there were certain foods she knew she couldn't eat, her stomach wasn't always predictable when it came to what she could and couldn't have. Some-times she'd end up with the worst stomach pain.

In 1995, she had blood in her stool, and that worried us, so we ar-ranged for her to see a gastrointestinal doctor. This was during her se-nior year in high school. The doctor ordered a colonoscopy, and while they did find a few polyps, they couldn't zero in on a particular diagno-sis. Maybe it was diverticulitis? Maybe colitis? Maybe irritable bowel syndrome? Whatever the case, it wouldn't clear up, but she managed. That's one thing we always knew about Becky — she wouldn't give up.

Becky married John, and we were singing a lot. Then she got pregnant with Levi, and her stomach issues didn't go away, but they became less aggressive. That was a surprise, and she seemed better for years, with fewer symptoms. After she gave birth to Jakobi in 2000, she got really sick.

Her stomach issues started up again, and that wasn't the worst of it. She woke up one morning while we were on the road with a terrible headache, like a migraine but worse. Getting ready to sing, her eyes were bloodshot, and the headache seemed to settle in behind her eyes. It just kept getting worse, so we took her to the ER, and they gave her some pain meds and put her on an IV. Her headache calmed down a bit, and when she left, the ER doctor told her she should see an eye specialist.

When we got home, she followed up with an eye specialist, and they had all sorts of guesses as to what was going on, but still no one could give her a concrete reason for her pain. She came home, and things continued to get worse. The pain and headaches were almost unbearable, so bad that she would have to lie down with heat pads or ice packs on her forehead and eyes.

Through all of this, she kept singing. It's so hard to see your child suffering, and I wanted to make it all better for her, but no one could tell us what was wrong, much less what the cure might be. Night after night, we took the stage, and night after night, she could barely get through each performance. I wondered if she was going to have to take a sabbatical.

Then something even more weird started happening: When she got out of the shower, she felt like her legs were on fire. Sonya would have to fan Becky while she laid there in agony. We tried another doctor, with no new results.

A friend of ours mentioned the Mayo Clinic, and after a doctor referred her to them, she was able to fly out with John for a few days and undergo some tests. That's where she finally received a diagnosis: Crohn's Disease. It's an inflammatory bowel disease that causes inflammation to flare up in various parts of your digestive track. But Becky had a rare form of Crohn's that didn't only settle in her digestive system — it was moving around her body, causing inflammation behind her eyes and in the nerve endings of her skin.

The doctors there prescribed a type of chemotherapy shot that would help some of her symptoms subside, but as the months passed, they had to keep increasing the dosage to keep her symptoms under control. In 2004, it got to the point where the shots weren't even doing anything for her, so they added Humira. This medication is very severe — it helps limit inflammation by blocking part of your immune system, leaving you open to various infections and, in some cases, cancer.

By 2005, she had to alternate between chemo one week and Humira the next week. It was hard on her, and her anxiety levels were through the roof. We'd arrive at a venue to perform, and when it came time to man the merchandise table, Becky would get so nervous that she'd disappear. It was so unlike her — she normally loved mingling with people. She was the first person to go to bed and the last person to wake up. I was so worried about her.

One night we were playing in front of a large crowd and in the middle of a song, Becky turned around and stared at me, her eyes wide open, panic-stricken. I looked back at her, and we both kept singing. I didn't know what she wanted me to do. I didn't know what to do. Should we stop the concert? Should I tell Ben? Should Becky take a break? It was really scary.

Afterwards, when we had loaded up our equipment and the bus pulled slowly from the venue, I asked Becky what had happened.

"Mom," she said, "if I look at you again, just get close to me. We don't have to stop singing, but I need you to be near to me. I felt like I was going to faint."

I can't tell you how many times she looked at me that way on stage in the coming months. We would be in the middle of a song, and Becky would turn and look at me, her eyes reminding me so much of when she was a frightened little girl. And whenever she did, I would wander over towards her, not making a big production out of it. I'd ease up behind her, and we would all keep singing, and I would pat her on the back, just standing there with her, reassuring her I was there. She never did pass out.

This was a hard season. We had ice packs in the freezer at all times to help with her headaches, and she wore tinted glasses so people wouldn't see her bloodshot eyes and ask questions. Whenever she took the stage, she identified the quickest ways to get backstage. We didn't know what else to do.

Perhaps the worst part was that I could tell Becky was beginning to second-guess herself. We tried to encourage her to keep going. She was so talented but dreaded playing. I wondered how much longer we could go on like that.

We stopped at the Mall of America in Minnesota during one of our weekend trips on our way to Canada. It was a big day, we were en route, and we didn't have any other stops to make, so we were all looking forward to unwinding a bit and walking around one of the largest shopping malls in the country. We planned to spend the entire day there.

The place is massive, and we started off together but eventually went our separate ways. That's when Becky called me.

"Hello?" I said into my phone.

I could barely hear what she was saying.

"Becky? What's wrong? I can't hear you."

She was in another store, having some serious trouble. She had been unable to eat or digest anything for three days, and she felt awful.

"Mom," she said quietly. "What am I going to do?"

I went and found her, and we made our way back to the bus.

~ ~ ~ ~ ~

There are few things worse than that feeling of helplessness you have when one of your children is suffering and there's nothing you can do about it. When you've gone to countless doctors and no one can offer you answers or hope; when you've sat beside your child's bed, holding their hand and hoping they can fall asleep; when you have watched them throw up because they're in so much pain; it is an awful thing, that helplessness.

Then, a breath of hope.

A friend of a friend knew what Becky was going through and told her about this holistic clinic she had heard amazing things about.

Becky was on the fence. We had never heard of it, and we weren't sure how we felt about taking her problems outside of the traditional medical field. She was in bad shape, but we didn't want to make it worse.

We still lived in East Tennessee at that point, and this clinic was in Nashville.

"If you want to go and check it out," I told Becky, "I'll go with you."

We told Sonya what we were thinking and arranged to spend the night with her. Becky decided to give it a try. She had nothing to lose at that point. Why not?

The two of us went to the clinic and met with the woman who ran it. They did multiple examinations and ran a battery of tests. After those were finished, we met with the head of the clinic again.

"Usually, when we do tests, we schedule another appointment a few days later to go over the results, but since you're here from out of town, why don't you go out and have some lunch, then come back this afternoon and I can go over the results with you?"

She was so kind. Becky and I went out to lunch, excited to see what the results might be.

When we returned, sitting down in the woman's office, I was feeling nervous but also hopeful. What if this proved to be a breakthrough for Becky? What if they could actually pinpoint the problem and give her something to help?

Before Becky had a chance to tell the woman all of her symptoms, the woman pulled out Becky's results and told us, point by point, what Becky was probably experiencing, her pain and her discomfort and even her anxiety. She read Becky like a book. And she was right in every respect. It was amazing. She went back over Becky's symptoms and explained why she thought they were taking place.

It felt like a picture of Becky's health was emerging.

"I think I can help you," the woman said in a quiet, confident voice.

The regimen the woman recommended was expensive, so Becky went outside and called John to see what he thought about it.

"We have nothing to lose," he said. "Do it. Try it."

For the next few months, Becky saw improvement. Then, within a year, she experienced major improvement. Now, she's been nine years without any sign of a Crohn's flare-up, without any of the intestinal issues she used to struggle with.

What an amazing thing.

~ ~ ~ ~ ~

I still remember one date in particular in 1998, before Becky got the help she needed, when we were singing in front of 10,000 people, and Becky was so upset prior to going onstage that I didn't think she'd be able to do it. She was having anxiety attacks that were nearly crippling, but somehow, she got out on that stage and performed. The week after that, we did the Ryman, also without Sonya, and again Becky fought through the anxiety, barely able to breathe, nearly getting sick on stage. But she did it, and she sang beautifully. I'm so proud of her for what she did during that time. I'm proud of all of us — Ben really stepped up and became a steady rock we could all lean on.

After she learned to cope with her anxiety and her health improved, Becky started dreaming up bigger dreams. She started wondering if maybe she might be able to try some different things musically. Becky always found her comfort zone in being with the family on stage. She is more quiet than the rest of us, more reserved, and any time she has done a big event, it's been with us — the Gaither shows or Carnegie Hall or the Grand Ole Opry — and we've done some big arenas, sung the national anthem at ball games.

Around 2017, we happened to be on the same flight as Alison Krauss, a friend of ours, and Becky and Alison spent some time catching up. Soon after that, Alison had a show come up at the Bridgestone Arena where she would be doing one song for an event. She called Becky and asked if she would sing with her and play guitar. Ricky Skaggs would be on the same stage, along with Don Waz, Sam Bush, and Jamey Johnson.

Becky wasn't sure what to say.

Perform at Bridgestone Arena? With Alison Krauss? Singing and playing her guitar?

"Let me pray about it," she told Alison. For a week, Becky was beside herself. She knew she had to do it, knew it was an opportunity for her to overcome some of her fear and anxiety, but saying yes was tough.

"You can do it," I told her. "We'll be right there in the front."

She called Alison Krauss back.

"I'll do it," she said. "I'll do it."

That night at the Bridgestone, John, Jakobi, Levi, and I watched while she rehearsed with Alison. Then, before the actual concert, we prayed in the dressing room, held hands in a circle, and asked God to be with her.

That night, she took the stage with the band, walked out in front of that huge crowd with Alison Krauss and Ricky Skaggs, and she nailed it. I mean, she sang her part flawlessly. It was absolutely amazing watching her up there, thinking about how far she had come. She was doing the thing she feared the most, putting herself and her talent out there. It was an incredible moment.

~ ~ ~ ~ ~

During those early years after Joe left, Sonya, Becky, and Ben started picking out the songs they wanted to sing. That was when we entered a new chapter of The Isaacs, and the kids began writing more and more original material. I would listen to their new ideas, their new lyrics, and I gained a whole new appreciation for how incredible my children were. Their songs were amazing, and in the years to come, they would win many awards.

They were growing in more ways than only their songwriting. Sonya's time on the road with Vince Gill had given her a new confidence. Becky's time as the lead for our family had proven to her that she could do it, and she had a new air about her, one of confidence and courage. Ben became the man of the family, and he took on that role in a wonderful way. Of course, his two sisters are very outspoken, so they never let him get away with too much.

They were growing and maturing as musicians. It was a joy to watch. I had no idea that there would come an opportunity where they might have to leave me behind.

CHAPTER
3

Around 2006, my kids and I were on tour with the Gaithers, and the main production company they used at the time was Steve Moore's company, AEG. He was a big country music guy and a booking agent for some big names in the industry. During that tour, he became an Isaacs fan. He was friendly and very complimentary, and we enjoyed getting to know him.

One day before a show, he came into the dressing room to chat with us. "You guys are really different," he said, and we all laughed. "No, I mean that as a compliment. Seriously. Your sound is amazing. Have you ever thought about cutting a country record?"

We all sort of held our breath. Of course, we had thought about that, always wondered if there could be a niche for us singing clean country. Making a country record would definitely help expand our audience.

"It's something we've talked about," Ben said.

"I see a lot of potential with The Isaacs," Steve replied. "Your harmony, your look."

He paused, thinking, and we waited to see what he was going to say next. Finally, he asked: "What would you think about cutting a few sides, and then we could pitch it to a few labels, just kind of gauge if there's any interest?"

Wow. We were thrilled at the idea of making music with him, and we were honored that he saw something special in our group. I could feel the energy in the room, and we agreed to talk more about it in the coming weeks. I was excited about the possibilities, but I could tell my kids were even more excited.

Not too much later, we met up with Steve again. This was when I heard some hard news.

"Listen," Steve began, "we're really excited about the potential of The Isaacs in country music. I think you guys have what it takes. But it's important that you understand, in country the people are usually young, and they're very fickle about new acts. It's hard to break in and even harder to stay in."

He paused. When he said the word "young," I felt my heart in my throat. I was not old at the time, but I certainly wasn't young anymore.

"We feel like the primary image needs to be that of the three kids. Not that Lily can't sing with them, but all of the promotion and advertising needs to focus on the three kids. We think this will give you the best image and the best opportunity to succeed in country music."

They said it discreetly, in the midst of a lot of other thoughts and ideas, and they certainly spoke with kindness, but his words hit me sideways. It felt like a slap to the face. I was in my mid-50s, and I tried to keep up with the current fashions and trends. I didn't feel old, but my kids were in their early 30s. I understood. But that didn't mean I felt good about it.

I had worked all of my adult life, since we started in 1971, to promote our ministry and our career. I had given it 100% all the time: physically, financially, and emotionally. But here I was, being edged out, pushed to the periphery because I was older. That hurt. It was a real blow to the identity I had worked so hard over the years to create.

I nodded and smiled through the conversation with Steve, keeping a lot of my pain and insecurity inside because I didn't want my kids to be upset. I mean, they knew it hurt me, and they hated that I couldn't be front and center with them because they knew how much I had invested in making The Isaacs what it was. They knew how much I loved to perform with them, but there was nothing we could do about it. I didn't want to act like a baby, throw a fit and try to get my own way. I wanted to see my kids succeed.

So we worked with him to put together a 30-minute showcase. In our industry a showcase is a scheduled singing event where you rent a place and invite key industry people to come — record companies, booking agencies, those kinds of people. It was a small, intimate event with maybe 100 people there. We supplied some appetizers and tried to make it a comfortable environment.

The showcase was in a kind of coffee house. It had enough space for people to come and go, and it had a small stage. We arranged for it to take place around 5:30 or 6:00 p.m., just as people were getting out of work, so they could stop by, grab some appetizers and drinks, and listen to us sing. Steve invited four different labels, and while the crowd stayed relatively small, it was full of very influential country music decision-makers. We prepared six or seven songs that featured the kids — I wasn't pictured on any of the media photos.

When we sang in the showcase, I stood in the background. I knew they didn't want me to stand out, so I wore black to better blend in with the band, who also all wore black. It's hard to describe the mix of emotions I felt at the time, eager to see where it would all lead, feeling left out and pushed to the margins, embarrassed that I couldn't be singing with my kids and yet proud of how incredible they sounded.

The last song we sang was "It Is Well With My Soul," and, as usual, the kids nailed it. That really brought down the house, and the energy in the room was electric. If you've ever heard my kids sing that song, you know how powerful their voices are, how magical the harmonies. The silence that came in at the end felt holy, and then the crowd went wild. We spent a bit of time after that mingling with the crowd, getting to meet some of the executives, and talking about our history as musicians. There were so many compliments.

After the showcase, the waiting game. I felt like we had done the best we could do, and I was so happy with the kids' performance. Lo and behold, someone was interested in The Isaacs.

Out of that showcase, we were offered a developmental deal with Sony Records. They said they wanted to cut three or four songs to shop around, just to see how it would take. This wasn't an official signing, but they were willing to invest a little bit of money to see what might happen. Would the songs garner any interest? Would people jump on-board? Was it worth recording an entire album? These were the questions everyone wanted answers to.

It was an extremely exciting time for us. We had to do a promotional photo shoot, and two big producers got involved: Buddy Cannon and Mark Bright. I wasn't included in the photo shoot, and that hurt too. But there was nothing to be done, because I would never stand in the way of an opportunity for my children.

This feeling of being excluded actually led me to start writing out my story. What would I do if I wasn't singing anymore? I really had to consider that question, and the answer was nothing but silence and more questions. This is what I had been doing for over thirty years. I didn't know what else I could do. But I decided to write my first book, *You Don't Cry Out Loud,* and working through my own story was therapeutic and healing.

I met up with two friends whom I respected, Anne and Jonas Beiler. They came to East Tennessee to spend some time with me, and we talked for two or three hours. I didn't want to talk about it with just anyone — I don't think I even talked about it with the kids at the time, because I didn't want them to feel bad in any way.

But sitting there with Jonas and Anne, I cried and talked and cried some more, and it was so healing for me to get it out to someone who understood. I was embarrassed to say it hurt me that I couldn't be involved in this huge opportunity, but talking it out helped. Talking things out always helps.

For the next few months, we kept touring, the kids and me, doing our own dates. And they would spend the week in the studio, recording new tracks for Sony. I had to put it out of my mind. I had to stop worrying about the future, what might happen, where this path might lead us all.

But honestly? I became more and more devastated at the idea of The Isaacs changing, or at the thought of retiring, fading into the background. I kept praying, "God, your will be done. Your will be done. If it's time for me to pass the torch, to step aside, please give me the strength to do that, even though I still want to sing, even though I still want to perform every weekend."

As the weeks passed, the recording company got cold feet. There were two other sibling groups of three at the time that were coming on strong, and they didn't feel the time was right for another one. I also couldn't help but wonder if our gospel music background didn't have a negative impact. I don't know. Maybe that had nothing to do with it. In any case, it didn't fly, and we kept doing what we were doing. Of course, the children were disappointed, and I really was disappointed for them. We had hoped it would open up a lot of doors, but I guess it wasn't meant to be.

And I wouldn't have started writing my book if it wasn't for that big detour. I wonder about this a lot. I try to keep my eyes open now when disappointments come along. I try to see what new opportunities or paths they are leading me down.

That entire situation was such a difficult thing for my kids, and they treated me with such tenderness while we went through it. Once we were on the other side of the process, they became very deliberate about pulling me in, no matter the venue or opportunity. If anything happened after that in the country music world, they involved me, even if it was just me doing some harmony lines here or there.

We were asked to do the CMA Country Christmas that would be aired on ABC with Reba McEntire in December of 2019. This was such a big deal for us, because we had never been on national television like that before. She wanted all of us up there, right alongside her. She made us feel like we were the biggest stars in the world. And when we sang at the Dove Awards, my kids made me get up there with them and sing "It Is Well with My Soul."

When peace, like a river, attendeth my way,
When sorrows like sea billows roll;

Whatever my lot, Thou hast taught me to say,
It is well, it is well with my soul.

It is well with my soul,
It is well, it is well with my soul.

My children always pull me in. They love me well. They always include me, even though they don't have to do that.

All will be well.

It's hard when the thing you've helped to create grows beyond you. Maybe you have a family business and you know it's time to pass it on to the next generation. Maybe you are the pastor of a church, and it's time to let the younger crowd take the reins. Maybe your role in life is changing. Accept it. Embrace it.

If you don't, you might lose it all.

~ ~ ~ ~ ~

Life passes, and things change. We moved on as a band, and it always seemed like things were getting better and better. We traveled nearly every weekend, singing at two or three venues. I moved to Nashville, as did Becky and her family, and that made things easier on us when it came to coordinating travel and playing larger venues in Nashville. We were all in the same city finally, and life was good.

Then came 2014, a year unlike any other.

CHAPTER
4

It was July, 2014, and we were getting ready to sing at the Country Music Hall of Fame in Nashville, Tennessee. Because we all lived in Nashville by that time, there was no travel involved — we would simply meet up at the venue earlier in the day to get everything set up, get dressed, do the sound check, and then prepare for the show.

I was running around the house, trying to get everything together that I was responsible for when Ben called.

"Mom, something's come up that I have to take care of. I'm probably going to be late for the show tonight."

"Oh," I said, trying not to sound alarmed. "Okay. Like, 30 minutes late?"

He paused. "No, later than that. I'll need you all to do the setup without me. Do your best with the sound, and I'll do what I can when I get there. I'm not sure exactly when."

"Is everything okay?" I asked, wishing he would tell me more but not wanting to pry.

"Yeah, I'll just be there a little late, that's all. I have to take care of something."

"Oh, okay," I said again, trying to sound calm. But this was strange. I waited for an explanation, but none came, just a quick, "Bye,

Mom." It was totally out of character for Ben — he was never late, and he never pawned off his duties to other people. He always did the sound prep. And because he didn't say exactly what was going on, I was worried. Was something wrong with one of the children? With his wife? Or with him? Was his diabetes acting up? But if that were the case, he would tell us. Was he struggling with something? My mind kept spinning, but I couldn't figure it out. He was a perfectionist, always made sure our sound was great, especially at the Country Music Hall of Fame.

I called Becky and Sonya, and we were all puzzled. Normally, for a 7 p.m. show, we'll get there around 2 p.m., set up our gear, do a sound check, and then go get dressed, put on our makeup, and be ready to go. But on that day, we struggled through setup before he arrived. We had our sound engineer there to help out, and my grandson Levi knew what to do, but it was a little nerve-wracking trying to get it all right. Ben is an expert at sound, produces albums for other people, and is one of the best in the business.

He came rushing in at 4 p.m., looked over everything we had done, made a few tweaks, and didn't let on that anything serious was wrong. He seemed distracted, but to be honest, he had seemed that way for months. I figured that if he wanted me to know what was going on he'd tell me, so I didn't ask any questions.

We played the show, and it went well. The more I thought about it, the more I thought he must have gotten tied up at the studio or something like that. One of his clients must have needed more time, or maybe he had double-booked and needed a few extra hours to get caught up. Maybe it wasn't a big deal. But in my heart, I knew something was wrong, something out of the ordinary. Maybe guys are different. My daughters would have called and told me exactly what was going on and asked for prayer, and we would have cried together if needed, and supported each other. But Ben was independent. He didn't want to bother anyone. He kept things to himself.

But later that night, the truth about what was going on came out. I guess he had said something about it to Becky, and then Sonya walked in, so he told her, and then I found them, so he told me too. One of his family members had to be enrolled in a 30-day rehab program.

We were shocked. We had no idea this was even going on. We'd spent time together as a family, shared meals together, hung out during holidays, and never had I suspected that this person might have a problem. I felt terrible because I hadn't been more supportive. If I had known, I could have helped, somehow. Or at least that's what I told myself. It was so hard.

Ben sat there and told us everything that had happened during the previous year, how tough it had been, how they were trying to figure it out, to make the right decisions, to help the family move forward.

"And it's for 30 days?" I asked.

He nodded.

"Then we have to pray," I said, and the four of us did, right there.

~ ~ ~ ~ ~

I grew up with an alcoholic in my own house: my dad. But I was young and immature, and I was selfish about it. I never tried to see things from my dad's perspective, never tried to look deeper into the reasons he turned to the bottle for comfort. Maybe that's how most teenagers would be, I don't know, but I didn't recognize my dad's addiction as evidence of the pain he felt, of the horrific memories that haunted him. I just didn't want him to embarrass me in front of my friends, which he did on many occasions. I loved him, but I was ashamed of him. I wanted to fit in, and having a dad who showed up drunk to the swimming pool didn't accomplish that.

I remember often thinking that it wasn't fair that my father was an alcoholic because my friends' parents were, for the most part, very normal. Those parents always came to their children's plays, sports activities, and shows. They walked around on steady feet and had coherent conversations with other parents, and sometimes even with me. They never showed any discernible signs of weakness. Those parents were clear-eyed, seemed kind, and were always there.

My father was never there. Never. He worked through the night, drank when he wasn't working, and slept when he wasn't drinking. I remember one instance where my mom had to go to the hospital because my father was so drunk that he fell down the subway steps and cut his head wide open. A stranger found him, lying on the pavement, bleeding, and an ambulance rushed him to the hospital. My mother had to go and pick him up. When she asked me if I wanted to go with her, I declined, unable to bring myself to go and see what his alcoholism had done to him. When he came home, he had a long line of jagged stitches in his head. For weeks, they were a reminder to me of how different my family was, a constant chorus of voices saying, *You will never be like the other kids. You will never fit in.*

And even when he wasn't drunk, he didn't want to do anything. He preferred sitting at home in his armchair and staring at the wall. One of the few things we did together as a family was to go to the temple on holy days or for Jewish festivals. Now I know the reason he never wanted to do anything was because he was probably depressed. And as I've discovered more and more about what he went through in the Holocaust, it all makes sense. His story of survival is the most sobering thing that I've encountered in my adult life. But I didn't know that when I was a teenager, and I didn't think to ask the questions. I look back on myself at that age and am disappointed at my insensitivity. I wish I could have known and done more. I remember thinking to myself, "I will never be with anyone who does that."

My father's alcoholism became my dirty little secret, one I was terrified my friends would find out about. I couldn't talk about it with my mom — we didn't talk about that kind of stuff. I couldn't talk about it with my brother — he was still so young. I couldn't talk about it with my friends —they were the ones I was trying so hard to keep the secret from! My approach was to hide it, mask it, and pretend it didn't exist.

I think that this happens often in families who have a family member with an addiction of any kind, whether it be alcohol or drugs or pornography or over-eating or whatever it might be. You carry the shame of it, even though it's not you. You don't want people to know that you have someone in your life who is that vulnerable, that dependent. You see it as a weakness, one you'd rather keep hidden.

I think, too, that children who grow up around people with severe addictions have to grow up faster than most children. I had to kick into mature mode because of my father's actions and the results of his decisions. I held a lot inside. I had to convince my mother not to leave him. I had to protect my brother. I had responsibilities that no teenager should ever have. I made that choice. Just me.

The only outlet I had was my diary, the only "one" I could trust, the only one who wouldn't say anything no matter what I revealed.

But we have to share these things with someone. Writing these things down is good and healthy, but it's no substitute for actually talking about it. We have to allow others to come alongside us and help shoulder the load.

~ ~ ~ ~ ~

Ben was hurting, but he has always been very private, so he didn't want to burden us with what he was going through. And in many ways, it was personal, so he didn't want to share. I understood that, but I could tell the situation continued to bother him. He wasn't his normal jovial self. He was quieter, kept more to himself, and got agitated easier than he normally did. When we were all on the bus traveling together, I could tell when he woke up that he hadn't been sleeping well.

"Everything okay, Ben?" I asked him.

"It's okay, Mom," he said in a tired voice.

The girls and I tried to be as supportive as we could, sending things to the rehab center, letters and notes. We tried to help out with responsibilities around their house. We wanted to provide support.

One weekend, Ben couldn't travel with us because there was a family orientation to help prepare them for when their family member came home. When the big day finally came, we all reached out and said how proud we were, how happy, and how we all had high hopes. Everyone went to a celebration dinner one night, and it was a beautiful evening full of kindness and humility.

By the time August rolled around, other things were going on in the family. Sonya was pregnant, due in November, and my mother had moved to California, to an assisted living center that she seemed to be enjoying. It felt like everything was resolved and that there was hope for a peaceful future.

That went on for one month.

Ben called me on the phone one night after we got home from a trip and said that when he got back to his house, he found the family member. They had relapsed.

~ ~ ~ ~ ~

Seeing any of my children in pain is never easy. In fact, it's probably one of the hardest things about being a parent. I'll never get used to it, and I'll never stop wishing I could take on the pain in their place. Pastor Jim Cymbala once said to us while we were performing at the Brooklyn Tabernacle, "You're only as happy as one of your saddest children." And it's so true. If one of your children is in pain, that's how you feel.

Watching Ben go through this situation reminded me of when he was 17 years old. He had an incredible growth spurt at that age. He had always been tall, but he seemed to grow a foot that year, and at the same time, he lost some weight. He looked pale and complained about being thirsty a lot, woke up with cotton mouth, and seemed to be going to the bathroom all the time. By then I started to worry. I had recently read an article about the symptoms for diabetes, and I wondered if this was Ben's problem.

We made an appointment with the family doctor, and he had some blood tests run. His sugar came back at 490. Normal sugar levels are around 120. This was obviously a problem, so the doctor put him on some pills and recommended a particular diet.

"Let's try this for two weeks and then I'll see you again. Hopefully these adjustments will help get your insulin levels under control."

But when we returned two weeks later, nothing had changed, so he sent Ben to an endocrinologist for further testing. When we showed up there, it didn't take long for him to give Ben a diagnosis of diabetes.

"The pills don't seem to be doing enough," he told us. "You need to go on insulin shots."

In that moment, when the doctor said those words, I wished it were me. Ben was a diabetic at 17 years old, and it broke my heart. But what can you do? We sat there while the doctor showed Ben how to give himself the life-saving insulin shots. I turned my face away and cried.

As we gathered our things together and walked outside the doctor's office, Ben turned to me with a tired look in his eyes.

"I'm going to go take a drive, Mom," he said.

"Are you okay?"

"I'm fine," he said. "I just need to think. I need to be alone."

I cried all the way home. Ben was gone for a few hours, and I worried about him. Of course I did. And I waited for him to come home, as parents so often have to do. Sometimes our children have to leave us for a short time to figure life out.

He pulled up in his truck and came inside, and we stood there for a moment, talking about what this might mean for him.

"I don't know how my life is going to change," he said. "Not for sure. But why me? Why is this happening?"

And his words echoed in my mind for a long time after that.

Why me? Why is this happening?

Too often as a parent, I have not had the answers. I guess this is life.

I hated his diabetes. I hated it. I know people have to deal with it, millions of people, but it was so hard to watch him as he went from giving himself one shot to two shots to four shots per day. And every time he took a shot, he had to eat. It killed me that he was going through it, but he handled it really well (maybe better than I did). He became very responsible, sticking to the diet the doctors gave him and going to all of his appointments. He did so well with it that few people even knew he was a diabetic.

Fifteen or twenty years ago he was fitted with an insulin pump, which changed his life. No more shots. He exercises and watches what he eats. To this day, if he feels a little weak on stage, he has to go to the bus and eat an apple with some peanut butter. But he takes such good care of himself.

Watching him go through this struggle with his family member, watching him try to live a life, be a good husband and father, and make difficult decisions while someone he loved fought alcoholism, it took me back to what it was like watching him suffer in those early days of his diabetes diagnosis. It wasn't easy. But I knew he would be okay.

~ ~ ~ ~ ~

After my divorce, Ben took on many of the burdens of the ministry — he picked up maintenance of the bus, took over the sound system, became the man of the family in many regards. It was a lot on him. So, as the seriousness of his family member's situation settled in on all of us, I worried about his health.

"I just don't know what to do," he said quietly. My strong son was reaching the end of his rope. He reached out to a counselor and received good advice. But the back and forth went on for months with this family member, being clean and relapsing, trying hard to keep it together and then falling apart.

Ben tried to stay strong, but I could see it was wearing on him. What could we do? We all felt helpless. I didn't want to get in his face or prod him for more information. I didn't want to come off as nosy. I wanted to hold him, like I did when he was my little boy, but I couldn't do that.

"We're on your side," I told him. "We're praying for you all. We know it will work out. We love you. If you need to take a sabbatical, we'll figure it out."

In 2016, something clicked, and Ben's family member has been clean ever since. But when Ben shares the story at our concerts, he says he still battles to keep hope in the midst of fear.

"It's like you're walking on glass," he will often say, "even after all this time. Because I remember what it was like. I still battle that."

Hope and fear. Hope and fear. Can they live in your heart at the same time? It's a battle. I hate to write this, but in many areas of my life I am an anxious person. I often wake up in the morning unsettled, concerned about the future, worrying over this thing or that. I fear things I really shouldn't worry about and have no control over. Whenever I feel a strange lump in my body or don't feel well, I fear my cancer coming back again. I am nervous when a tornado watch is issued, and if it's stormy outside, I'm reminded that I don't have a basement. I live more carefully than I used to.

I worry about holding up my kids if something were to happen that left me bedridden, or if I require care in my old age. I don't want to be a burden on them. If I had a spouse, I would have someone else to depend on. If you love someone like that and they love you back, you know they'll take care of you. But I don't want my children to have to take care of me.

I think it's important to talk about your fears. When we share them with someone else, often the fear melts away.

During a recent Christmas, the whole family got together — me and the kids and their spouses and the grandchildren. We have a tradition at Christmas, that when we're all together at my house, we gather in the living room and everyone says one thing they're especially grateful for from the previous year. Even the kids. It's become a really beautiful tradition.

And during this recent Christmas, Ben's family member told us what they were thankful for.

"I just want to thank the family for all of your support. I'm sorry for any hardship that I caused any of you. I'm just so glad to be part of this family."

We were all in tears.

"I'm proud of you," I said.

We've come through a lot. But that was only the first difficult thing we had to journey through together during 2014. I had no idea at the time that my mother was about to take a turn for the worse.

CHAPTER
5

L ily? Lily, I want to go home. Lily? Are you there? Are you there? Lily, I don't want to stay here. I want to go home. Okay. She's not here. I'm just talking, and she's not answering."

When Mom was widowed for the second time, my brother and I gave her a choice because we didn't want her living alone in New York any longer. It was too dangerous for her at 90 years old, so we gave her a choice between Tennessee or California, and she chose California because there was a larger Jewish population, and she was familiar with the synagogue there.

I smiled sadly to myself as I stopped listening to my voicemail and boarded our touring bus. It was September, 2014, and my mother had left me yet another message from her assisted living facility. Every single night at around 6:00 Pacific time, she called, and if I wasn't on stage I would answer and we would chat for a few minutes. It was like she couldn't go to sleep until she heard my voice. I guess there was something about chatting with me that kept her wandering mind in place. For me, it was a welcome way to mark the passing days, just chatting with my mom.

On the nights I didn't answer, she'd leave short messages. Sometimes it was just her voice trying to find me, sometimes she told me about her day, and — these were the worst — sometimes she was in distress, desperately wanting to go back to her home in New York City. The messages didn't always make sense. She was 95 years old by then, and while she was normally able to stay grounded in reality, her occasional lapses into a world she made up in her mind concerned me. I was deeply concerned she might be coming down with dementia.

Dementia is one of the most unsettling things because you can't function without your brain. It controls your speech, your memory, and every organ that works in your body. Losing a sense of who you are and what you want to say is a terrifying prospect. To hear my mom make senseless comments, and her being in that state of confusion so often, worried me. It made me sad, because up until that part of her life, she was so alert and active and remembered everything. She was articulate about her feelings. It put me in a lonely place to think that the next time I visited her, she might not know who I was. As she talked to me more and more in these rambling sentences, I knew something serious was wrong.

I hated to lose her that way.

On the nights when it wasn't too late, I called her back, but on that particular night in September, her message reached me long after I thought she would be in bed. I had just gotten out of a concert and we were packing our things, getting the bus and the trailer ready for a long drive to our next engagement. My daughters and I were busy getting settled in the bus, and Ben was making sure all the equipment was loaded properly. It was late, and I was tired.

Everywhere we go these days, we have loyal fans and old friends, and it was a good evening of singing and catching up. It's amazing to me how this little Jewish girl (me!) who grew up in New York City, married a hillbilly from Kentucky, and raised three children can now have friends around the world, all because of our family's singing. It just goes to show that you never really know how things are going to turn out. You never know how God is going to use you.

My mother had taken a serious fall only two months before that, in July, and afterwards we had been forced to move her to three different assisted living communities as her health continued to decline. For two months, she lived with my brother until there was a free room. The first place was a beautiful home in downtown San Francisco where 90% of the people were Jewish Holocaust survivors. Mother was a smoker for 70 years, and when we moved her there, because smoking was not allowed, my brother took her cigarettes. But she was still hiding cigarettes everywhere in his house, even in pockets of his clothing and under the bed, so eventually he managed to get her to quit cold turkey. For a little while after that, he would call and threaten to send her to Tennessee because, in his words, he was "living with the devil." He had his hands full, but I have to laugh at that situation now because she was quite a character.

During this time, I flew to New York to pick her up and help her pack, and the next day we went to the airport to head to Miami where she planned to stay for three weeks. This was around 2008. She was already widowed from my stepfather and enjoyed going to Florida for a short time in the winter. I was making sure she had everything she needed, and when we arrived at the airport, we went through security. I told her to make sure she didn't have her lighter and cigarettes in her carry-on.

Anyway, we made the trip and everything was fine. After I got back home, a week later, when I was getting ready to go on tour, I opened up one of my carry-ons that I had taken on that trip with Mom, and I found her lighter and cigarettes stuffed in one of the three pockets of that bag! I laughed out loud and said to myself, *That feisty scoundrel!* She had put her stuff in my bags, and I don't know how I got through security twice with that lighter in there.

After taking a few months to get adjusted, Mother was very happy there. She made a best friend whose name was Millie. The two of them were inseparable, going to the movies together, playing bingo together, sitting together for supper. It was really nice, and she was content. She was there for probably around two years when we got a call from management, and they said my mother was doing some abnormal things. It concerned them, so they wanted us to come in for a meeting.

The next week I scheduled a flight to San Francisco, and my brother and I spoke with the manager and a couple of the nurses. They told us mother was showing signs of dementia because she had tried to flush a towel down the toilet, and it blocked up all of the plumbing in the building. She also sat in the dining room and shouted at the server, becoming irate that they had brought the wrong food, even when the correct meals had been given to her. They said they had to either release her or move her into the Alzheimer's unit. She liked the place she was in and had made friends. We didn't want to move her from that facility.

My brother and I walked through the Alzheimer's unit, and it was probably the most sobering thing I've ever seen. Walking down the hallway, we saw residents who were sitting in their wheelchairs, emotionless, with a faraway look in their eyes, sitting in their beds without moving. It felt like a death sentence for my mother, because she was still active, loved to hold conversations, dance, put together her wardrobe, and put lipstick on. She still enjoyed life. She was a social butterfly. Even though she was confused, we didn't think that was the right place for her, so we opted to move her from that assisted living facility.

Within a month, my brother found a place for her in Novato, fifteen minutes from his home. It took her a while to get used to it, but she did. And it was certainly easier for him to go see her on a daily basis. During this entire time, we had someone come in the home a couple of hours every day to give her company and take her out. Then one day she decided to take a walk, and someone found her trying to cross the street in front of the assisted living building. That happened twice, so once again, we had to move her to a more secure facility, where she stayed for the rest of her life.

Each move seemed to take a toll on her memory and her ability to get around on her own. She had to make new friends and find her way around. Suddenly, getting from her bedroom to the dining hall was a challenge for her. At the most recent home, she would sometimes forget to put on her clothes for the day, and more than once she went into the dining room in her pajamas. This was one of the most alarming things to me because it showed just how far away she was from who she used to be. My mother loved dressing up, and for as long as I could remember, she kept meticulous care of her appearance. For her to leave her room and go to eat a meal with other people without looking her best, well, it was almost unimaginable to me.

After her fall in July, we took her to the doctor for x-rays. They didn't find anything wrong, but she lived with a lot of pain after that, and despite a regular regimen of Tylenol and ice, her discomfort never seemed to subside. I saw her later that summer, a few weeks after her fall, and she was still struggling. She got around with her walker but continued talking about the pain she was in. She moved around slower than usual. We didn't know what to do.

It was hard, seeing my mom fade so quickly. All of a sudden her clothes didn't match. She hadn't combed her hair. And for the first time in my life, I saw her walk out of her room without any rouge or lipstick. She had been strong late into her life, and for a long time it felt like she would never die. It felt like she would go on living indefinitely, always there for me to talk to. She had lived such a vibrant life, but my brother and I could tell she was getting close to the end.

This was the backdrop for all of the phone calls I received from her, all the heartbreaking messages. I still have them on my phone to-day. It came during the same year that Ben's family member was struggling. I think we were doing all that we could just to get by and stay above water.

~ ~ ~ ~ ~

On that night in September, as the bus rolled down the highway, I listened to her voice one more time.

"Lily? Lily, I want to go home. Lily? Are you there? Are you there? Lily, I don't want to stay here. I want to go home. Okay. She's not here. I'm just talking, and she's not answering." She was at the front desk of the assisted living place asking them to call her a cab. She thought she was in New York, but she hadn't lived there for three years.

It made my heart ache that she had to stay somewhere she didn't want to stay, that her life in New York was behind her, that she was getting closer and closer to the end. All of those years in her apartment, many with my father, my brother, and me. Many with only my father. Many with her second husband. And many years on her own. She had lived such a long and incredible life.

What would I do without her? I wiped tears from my eyes.

Lily, I don't want to stay here. I want to go home.

~ ~ ~ ~ ~

The next night, on September 20th, we were singing in Greensboro with the Gaithers. It also happened to be my birthday, and spending time with the Homecoming crew was a wonderful birthday present. It was a great show. We all sang our hearts out and had fun, as we always do. By the time we exited the stage and headed for the bus, it was late.

I turned on my phone, expecting to see a voice message from my mother, but instead I was greeted by a long list of missed calls from my brother. Since Mom lived near him, he took care of a lot of her daily needs and had the opportunity to visit her often. He'd take her out for a cup of coffee or take her to his house for a day, and I've always been grateful he got to spend that time with her. I always felt bad that I couldn't be more help, but I visited as often as I could.

His voice in the message made my heart drop. Somehow that night, while Mom was in the bathroom, she had fallen again. It was a serious accident, and they thought she had perhaps refractured whatever it was she had hurt in July. I called him immediately, concern numbing me.

"Hymie! What's wrong? What happened?"

After giving me the details of her fall, he said, "They took her into the emergency room. She will have to have surgery at 7 a.m. in the morning."

Surgery? She was 95 years old! I had to be there. I had to be with her. What if something went wrong? I would never forgive myself if I didn't get to see her again.

"What are they saying?" I asked him, feeling myself grow frantic with worry. "What do the doctors think?"

He paused, and the silence on the phone gave me knots in my stomach. My kids came over and sat beside me in the bus, aware that something serious was happening.

"Lily," my brother said, "the doctor warned us that at her age, her heart might not make it through the surgery."

She might not make it. Those words took my breath away. I pictured her lying there in a hospital bed, asleep in the night, waiting for surgery in the morning. She was so old, so frail. I wondered if she was afraid, if she even knew what was going on. I wondered if she was thinking of me. I missed her voicemail messages.

Oh, Mom.

The place where we had performed that night was in the middle of nowhere, but I managed to get online and book a flight out at 5:00 the next morning, the earliest flight I could find at the closest airport to our route. My family dropped me off at the airport at 1 a.m., and I walked inside, alone, sad, and worried. I didn't think I would ever see my mother alive again. She was so weak, and I couldn't imagine her making it through the surgery. But I prayed and prayed she could hang on until I got there.

Walking through the empty airport, I thought about all the times I had found myself in a similar situation: struggling, hurting, and on my own. My family has been so important to me, and they have been wonderful, but I wonder sometimes if God puts us in these situations where we have no one else to rely on except for Him. I remembered other times in my life when I had felt alone: that first Christmas after my divorce, finding out my cancer had come back, the time my children were approached to make a country album... without me.

But as I thought through those times of loneliness, I also remembered how God had met me. He had never left me alone. No matter how low I had been or how sad or lonely, God was right there in it. He will never leave me. He will never forsake me. The same can be said for you — He will never leave you. He will never forsake you. If you are in a time of deep loneliness, darkness, or despair, seek Him out. Look for Him. He is there with you.

The airport was quiet, which was strange. I've rarely been in an airport when there aren't other people there. But this was a small airport in the dark hours of the morning. All the stores were closed. A janitor made his way down the long hall, slowly mopping the tile floor. The luggage belts were still and empty. I found a place to sit and wait for the airport to open, and my children texted me every five minutes to make sure I was safe and everything was going okay. Their messages kept me occupied. I smiled to myself, wondering what I would do without my children. I don't think they slept all night.

One other person came in early, a nice man who was also waiting for a 5 a.m. flight. He was in his 60s or 70s, and he told me about his family, his life. We had a good conversation and it helped pass the time. The longer we talked, the faster the hours passed, and I really believed that God had placed him there, just for me. His presence was a gift.

The hours passed that way, in conversation with this stranger and in texts sent back and forth to my children and in prayers whispered to my Heavenly Father, and eventually it came time for me to board. I let my brother know I was on my way. Then I turned off my phone. That was hard, giving up all communication and settling in for the six-hour flight. We had to change planes in Charlotte, and I turned on my phone there. I spoke quickly with my brother. He was at the hospital waiting with Mother for her surgery, and he said she hadn't been taken back yet. Then it was back in the air, and I was nervous the entire time, praying God would let my mom live until I got out there to see her. As soon as the plane landed in San Francisco, I turned on my phone again and eagerly checked my messages.

She was alive. She had made it through surgery. The doctors had needed to implant screws in her hip in an attempt to heal what she had hurt in her fall. She was in recovery now. I had been awake all night, but I was determined to see her right away, so I hopped in a rental car and drove straight to the hospital.

When I walked into the room, my mom was still asleep. My brother and sister-in-law were there with her, such faithful companions. I put my hands up to my face and started crying when I saw her lying there, out of it, so small in that big bed. I just couldn't help it. I felt so relieved to have made it, so thankful she had survived her surgery, and besides that, I was exhausted. She had an IV in for fluids and was still receiving morphine, so she was out of it most of the time, and during the few times when she did wake up, she was confused. She didn't know where she was, and when I explained that she was in a hospital, she didn't understand why she was there. She wanted to leave. She wanted to go home — although she didn't have the energy to argue too hard about it.

When she spoke, she spoke in Yiddish, as if she had gone back 90 years to her childhood. Hearing her speak in her Jewish tongue took me back to my own childhood and those hot summer days in New York — the apartment I grew up in; those nights when I would lie in bed, listening to the city sounds outside my window, flinching under the harsh sound of my parents fighting, and dreaming of getting away, out into the world. There in the hospital, she spoke her Yiddish quietly, almost a whisper, and I had to lean in close to hear what she was saying. I was so glad that I still remembered the Yiddish she had taught me, that the two of us had spoken it sometimes with one another. I never would have understood so much of what she said in her last days if I didn't know Yiddish.

I think there is something especially heartbreaking when a child is there for the final days of her mother's life on Earth. That connection is so sacred, so important. I thought about the life she had given me, and what a life it had been — how she had carried me in her womb in the displaced-persons camp in Germany so soon after the horrors of the Holocaust; how she had cared for me in my younger years in New York City — feeding me and sending me off to school; how she had looked after me and tried to help me make it through those difficult teenage years, a time filled with boys and school and my dreams of becoming an actor and then a musician.

Now the tables were turned. My mother could not take care of me any longer — my brother and I were taking care of her. But just by being alive, just by her existence as my mother, I could still feel her thoughts towards me, her motherly affection, her desire for me to be happy and content and successful. It was hard to believe I might be losing that. It was hard to believe that my mother, my only mother, might be dying.

My brother had to go to work, so I was sometimes there with her by myself, just me and her. The nurses were fantastic, the doctors were great, and after two days, they took her off the IV. But she wouldn't drink anything. We couldn't get her to take a sip of anything. Nothing! We even tried baby food, but she would weakly spit it out. We fought with her just to get a straw in her mouth, but she refused to swallow anything — no juice, no lukewarm tea (her favorite), no water. We asked the doctors if they would put her fluid IV back in. I was sure she wouldn't last long if she didn't get something in her, at least fluids, and I was a little frustrated that she was being so stubborn. Just drink something, Mother!

"We can't keep her on an IV indefinitely," the doctor told us. "She's 95 years old, and if she's forgotten, or refuses, to swallow, there's not much we can do."

I was frustrated that the doctors were giving up on her. I felt like they were signing her death certificate, like they were walking away from her without fighting. But there really was nothing we could do. If she wasn't going to try for herself, I couldn't try for her.

It felt like things were getting bad, and the doctor recommended we call hospice. My kids had moved on to the next show, the National Quartet Convention in Pigeon Forge, Tennessee. They were scheduled to sing in front of 10,000 people, so they couldn't leave, and they were so busy at the event and had poor cell phone service, so we couldn't talk much. My brother and sister-in-law practice Judaism, so they don't believe in Jesus the way I do. I felt like my Christian support network was down, and I didn't know how to pray or what to pray for. Again, I felt very much alone.

But Becky's husband, John, was at home, and I spoke with him a couple of times each day on the phone. He talked me out of the panic I felt, the loneliness, the hopelessness. I knew I had to be strong, but it was hard. I didn't want to let my mother go, and sometimes felt a panic rising at the thought of her dying, leaving me. Several times, when I was driving to the hospital, John prayed with me and talked me out of that dark place. He was such a strong support, another gift from God.

Never will I leave you. Never will I forsake you. I knew what that verse meant that night.

As it became more and more clear that these were my mother's last days, my main concern became praying over her before she died. We had conversations about prayer in the past, and they had never gone very well. Her deep, traditional Jewish heritage resisted many of the things I had come to believe. I wanted one last chance to share the peace and hope of Yeshua our Savior, our Redeemer, with her.

Sunday turned into Monday turned into Tuesday turned into Wednesday, the days blurring together, the weariness going into my bones. She was in and out of sleep, always speaking quietly in Yiddish whenever she spoke. I kept trying to get her to drink water. I knew she needed it. But I was also praying that I could share the Lord, the living water she needed.

One time, when my mom woke up, she said something that alarmed me. She was really struggling to speak.

"What, Mom?" I asked, getting close to her again. "What do you need?"

"Ich chub nisht keyn koech," she said in Yiddish, and the frailness of her voice broke my heart all over again. "I have no strength."

This was not the strong mother I remembered from years gone by, the one who had survived the Holocaust, the one who had survived concentration camps, the one who had lost so many family members, the one who had married and moved to New York and made a life for herself. She had a hard life and was stuck in a marriage, but she dreamed big, made it work, gave up everything for us, and loved my brother and me unconditionally. And now she was too weak to eat or drink. Her physical strength was failing her.

"Don't worry, Mom," I said. "You don't have to have strength. Just relax, go back to sleep. You'll be okay. You just need to rest."

Within a few minutes, she gathered herself and spoke again.

"I'll miss you."

"What did you say?" I asked, getting in as close to her as I could. "I'll miss you," she whispered again. She closed her eyes and went back to sleep.

I went over to my chair, sat down, and wept.

Oh, my God, I prayed. *Is this really happening?*

I went back to my brother's house that night to sleep, and I told him what she had said, but he said it didn't mean anything for sure. Yet I felt like she knew the end was coming. He didn't think it was a big deal, dismissed it, and that upset me. I felt alone, isolated in knowing that the end was coming for Mom, and there was no one to stand with me in that hard reality. When she had said, "I'll miss you," I had sensed something in her, something that was preparing for the end.

I was so troubled and anxious, and I felt really alone. I needed to get into a corner somewhere and just pray to my Heavenly Father. I needed to be comforted by His Holy Spirit. There was only so much I could do by talking with family. So there I was, on an air mattress in the middle of my brother's living room. When all the lights went out, I began to weep. The thought of losing my mother was devastating enough, but not having my support team with me made me feel the loneliest I had ever felt. At that point, I knew what I had in my heart. I knew my relationship with God. I knew I was the bride of Christ. But I had to start lacing up those combat boots again, because it was inevitable that my mom would die.

And I had to be strong.

Somewhere, somehow, I knew I had to be alone with her.

I knew I had to pray with her. I knew she was on her way home.

~ ~ ~ ~ ~

On Wednesday, they said they couldn't keep her in the hospital any longer. There was nothing they could do. She needed to return to assisted living.

That was also the week my first book released, *You Don't Cry Out Loud,* and my publisher had arranged a special event for me at a retail convention to promote my book. I couldn't leave my mom, so my kids did it for me. Sonya read two sections from the book and they sang two songs on my behalf. I was so sick I had to miss it, but they took care of it for me, and, as usual, they did wonderfully.

On Thursday morning, the 25th, they moved her back to assisted living. They fixed up a hospital bed for her. She was confused and weak and didn't realize what was going on. It was a busy day, and then hospice arrived.

"Just because we're here," one of them told me, "it doesn't mean she's going to die anytime soon. She could live for months! She won't walk again, but she might live on for some time."

I didn't want to lose her, but I also couldn't imagine my mother living that kind of a life for very long, confined to her bed, sleeping the days away, slowly losing her strength. Once upon a time, she had been the liveliest of women, a spitfire during the day and out dancing at night! She had never let anything stop her or get in between her and a life full of joy and fun and excitement. I spent all day Thursday trying to make her comfortable and get her settled in. I stayed with her until my brother came in that night. My niece and nephew were there, and I didn't leave right away, but I didn't know what to say to her or if she'd even understand me, and if she did understand me, I didn't know how to pray over her without offending or upsetting her.

I especially didn't want to talk about it with her around my family, because it was a touchy subject. When I first decided to believe in Yeshua as my Messiah, a distance had settled in between me and the rest of my Jewish family, and that was hard. It lasted a long time. When they found out, they disowned me and said they never wanted to see me again. I had become the black sheep of the family. I didn't want to bring all of that pain and hurt back up for them during the last days or hours of my mother's life.

On Friday morning, I woke up and went back to the hospital. I usually arrived around 10 a.m. That morning, when I woke up, something told me to take my Bible, a small copy I carry with me when I'm traveling. So I stuffed it in my purse, but after that I didn't think much of it.

I got to her room and walked in. It was still early, and the blinds were closed, so the room was dark. Mom was in the bed sleeping with her mouth open. There was juice and water on her bedside table, but I could tell she hadn't touched it. They said she had forgotten how to swallow. I sat down in my chair, close to the bed, and waited. I prayed and I cried.

At 11 a.m., I was there alone with her, and I felt the Lord speak to my spirit.

Open your Bible. Just let it fall open.

I did, and my Bible opened to Psalm 23. I took that as direction. This is what my mother needed to hear. I whispered into her ear, and I took her hand in mine. I read the entire chapter, calm and easy.

The LORD *is* my shepherd;
I shall not want.
He makes me to lie down in green pastures;
He leads me beside the still waters.
He restores my soul;
He leads me in the paths of righteousness
For His name's sake.
Yea, though I walk through the valley of the shadow of
        death,
I will fear no evil;
For You *are* with me;
Your rod and Your staff, they comfort me.
You prepare a table before me in the presence of my
        enemies;
You anoint my head with oil;
My cup runs over.
Surely goodness and mercy shall follow me
All the days of my life;
And I will dwell in the house of the LORD
Forever.

When I finished reading Psalm 23 to her, I prayed again. How often I prayed during my mother's last days — for peace, for courage, for her to know she wasn't alone. I prayed she would know I was there with her. She had been there for me so many times in my life, and I didn't want her to feel like she was going through this last battle without me.

I was holding her hand and it was warm. I bent over her to kiss her on her forehead, and when I did, her face was freezing cold. So cold. Abnormally cold, in fact, and it scared me. I immediately ran out into the lobby and found one of the hospice nurses, and she came back into the room with me, along with another nurse.

They turned on the lights. They checked her pulse.

"Her breathing is shallow and her heart is beating very, very slowly," the nurse said. "I think she's going. It's just a matter of time now."

I stood there beside my mother with tears pouring down my face.

Lord, I prayed, *she had to hear my voice every night before she went to bed, and you gave me this precious gift of having time alone with her.*

"I was reading the Bible to her a few minutes ago," I told the nurse. "Do you think she heard me?"

"Yes," the nurse said. "Hearing is the last thing to go."

Thank you, Lord, for giving me the chance to read to her. Thank you that Psalm 23 is the last thing she heard.

As I was weeping, I pictured myself every night at 8 p.m. answering my phone, hearing Mom's voice, saying, "I love you." It was that two-minute conversation that gave her peace to sleep that night. She had to hear my voice every night, and now I was there for her one more time. This felt like the last 8 p.m. phone call.

I called my brother and told him she was dying, and he said he would come in right away. I called my children, and they video chatted to her on her deathbed, telling her they loved her. My children sang "It Is Well with My Soul." Of course, they were beside themselves. We were all so close to her. As tiny as she was, as weak as she had become, she was the face of resilience in our lives, always had been. She was a force unlike any other. And now she was leaving us.

I am so grateful God gave me that gift on the last day of her life, the gift of time to read scripture with her. To this day, I can hardly believe the Lord allowed me to do that. I had done the same thing with my father — we prayed for him, and he died the next day. We had stood at the edge of the cliff, right there at the edge, and God had been with us.

Again, I had to put on my combat boots. Again, I had to trudge through a difficult time in my life.

Little did I know, we would experience another significant loss in our family only a few weeks later.

CHAPTER
6

After Mother died, our schedules were crazy. There were preparations to be made for her funeral services, travel arrangements for my family to get to the West Coast, and we had to juggle some of our performance dates to make space for everything. I was so sad to have lost my mom, and I wondered if life would ever settle back down into something I recognized.

We gave Mother a complete Jewish funeral, burying her the day after she died because, traditionally, Jewish people do not embalm. A rabbi came to do the service, and Mother was buried in a white shroud. Her coffin was made of pine wood, white, and had a white Star of David engraved on top of it. It was simple, elegant, and reflected Mother's deep roots. I think she would have liked it.

At the funeral home, we asked if they could open the coffin for my children to see her, and they did. My brother opted not to see her like that, so it was just me, my children, and my grandchildren. She looked beautiful, so serene and peaceful. Again, memories swept over me: the feel of our apartment in New York City, the nights when I came home late from singing with my friend Maria, and the times my family would go back home and visit her, our children thrilled every time we entered the city. I imagined her at all these different times in her life: a young woman living in the concentration camps, or when she was newly married, or seeing her face in the crowd when I was performing in high school, or when we fought about leaving my dad. And I remembered the last time I saw her, in her hospital bed.

The Old Testament text used by the rabbi in his sermon at my mom's funeral was Psalm 23. He didn't know my story, didn't know how I had sat with my mom in her last moments on earth and read that psalm to her. He didn't know how much those words meant to me. But he read them, and he spoke about them, and it did my heart good. I just kept saying the last verse over and over again in my mind, even as I sat there listening, imagining my mom dwelling in the House of the Lord forever and ever. That's what gave me hope as I stood there listening.

I felt very much like a little girl again now that both of my parents had died. It's a strange feeling to know that the people who brought you into the world are no longer with you. Everyone goes through it eventually, and it's a really difficult emotion, a heartbreaking feeling. I felt like I was an orphan, and I've heard people say that before. When both of your parents have died, it's the strangest thing. I felt so alone.

What would it be like for me to be a mother to my children now that my own mother was gone? Being a mother has been the joy of my life. Before I had children, I wasn't convinced I could be the mothering type. I saw how being a mom came with a lot of challenges, a lot of pain, and a lot of constraints. I knew people who had children, and I saw how tied-down they had become. I was a free spirit. I had dreams and goals that reached far outside of any traditional kind of home. I was going to be a Broadway music star, the pride of my mother's and father's lives. If not, I'd become a famous folk singer, gracing stages all across the country. Those were my dreams! How could I possibly have children and still live the life I wanted to live? For a long time, I thought I would probably rather have a dog.

Before Ben was born, I had a normal job, serving as a secretary in an office. Joe and I had been married for a year, and my perspective on life was changing. I had friends who were couples with small children, church friends who gathered with their families, so we decided we'd try for a family.

When Ben was born, I took maternity leave, planning to spend at least a month or two with him before returning to my job. But it didn't take me long to realize I wanted to spend every second of every day with him. It was such a joy to be a mother, and that joy surprised me. Holding my infant baby boy in my arms was the most amazing emotional feeling I had ever experienced. This was an extension of my husband, myself, and our families. This boy was the firstborn American in my family, and my love for him was like nothing I had ever experienced. I loved being his mother.

Two years later, we had another child, my first baby girl, Sonya. I had a lot of complications with her. But she ended up being a healthy baby, and again I was amazed at my desire to mother.

Finally, one year later, we were surprised to have number three on the way. My baby Becky arrived.

I've spoken with mothers who have had one child, and when they find out their second child is on the way, they think there's no way they can love their second child as much as the first. This is such a common feeling. But somehow, your heart makes room for all of your children, and it's the same space, but your heart expands to engulf all of your children with the same love. When it's all said and done, your heart is big enough. How does that happen? It just happens.

What a busy time of life! I think I was exhausted 24 hours a day, even when I was sleeping. Being a stay-at-home mom consumed me, and because I didn't have anyone to help (Joe worked long hours and my parents were in New York, still upset with me for becoming a Christian), I took them everywhere I went. I became very attached to them. Children were my first priority in life. And as we all grew older, I wanted to be involved in everything they did.

As time went on, we remained close, probably closer than most parents are to their children. After all, we were together so much, traveling on the weekends to churches where Joe and I were singing. We performed together. We lived life in a tiny van together. And then, during the week, I had all of the normal duties associated with motherhood.

If I could say anything to today's mothers, it would be this: Listen to your children. Keep the lines of communication open with them, even if what they're saying sounds contrary to what you think or believe. Just let them talk. A lot of times, kids only need to vent. They want to get it out. If they don't ask for your opinion, just listen. Many times, I've seen doors close because parents give their opinions too quickly. I've been guilty of that. If they're opening up to you, it's a big deal.

My mother and I didn't talk a lot about life stuff. We just never had that kind of relationship. Most of the details about growing up as a young woman I learned from my friends. So, when I had children, I wanted to be the mother whom they would talk to about their problems and issues. I have always tried to listen without having an opinion.

That is my only advice to other mothers: Be a good listener.

~ ~ ~ ~ ~

As we walked in and sat down for my mother's funeral service, the realization hit me hard: My mother was gone. It almost took my breath away.

My niece and nephew both spoke at her funeral, and then each of my children said something as well. It is a strange and wonderful thing to hear your own children talk about your deceased mother. I was so proud of them.

I especially remember how Sonya got up at the front to say a few words. She was pregnant with her and Jimmy's next child, a little girl, and they planned on naming her Ayva Devorah after my mother, whose middle name was Devorah. In the Jewish tradition, you do not name your children after people who are still living, but you name them after those who have gone before you. Sonya said that she hoped their baby girl, the one she bore in her womb, would carry on the incredible legacy of my mother for another generation, and just thinking about that brought a smile to my face. I wondered what this little girl would be like with a name like that. Ayva Devorah. She would probably be full of life, as my mother was, feisty and determined and strong. I couldn't wait to meet her.

During the funeral procession, we walked behind Mom's casket, and the men in our family served as pallbearers. The cemetery was in Novato, just outside of San Francisco, and as we arrived at her gravesite, we stopped as a group, and the rabbi spoke. My girls and I sang the song, "My Yiddisher Mama." Singing with my girls in that moment was a holy experience, and for just a second, I caught a glimpse of eternity, where all of our generations would be reunited, where there will be no more death. It was so beautiful.

As her coffin was lowered slowly into the grave, the rabbi recited, "Al mekomah tavo veshalom," which means, "May she go to her place in peace." Once the coffin was lowered completely, everyone in the family took turns throwing dirt onto the casket. This is meant as an act of respect for the dead, or kevod ha-met. In every Jewish funeral, every family has an opportunity to take the shovel and throw dirt on the casket. It was a strangely peaceful thing to do and to watch my children and grandchildren helping with. Over and over again I thought of my mother and how much the ceremony would have meant to her.

While they were throwing dirt on the casket, I noticed there were four tombstones close to my mother's where U.S. veterans of WWII had been buried. Their gravestones surrounded her. How amazing, that even in death she was united with other WWII veterans. It's like they were still protecting her. I thought again of her experiences in Poland, how she had been a survivor! An overcomer! Someone who had lived her life full of joy and enthusiasm and faced every new adventure with determination.

When I walked away from her gravesite, I felt everything you can imagine: grief, loneliness, and relief that she was no longer suffering. I felt an intense sadness that she had been forced to live such a difficult life, and that she had experienced so much pain. God, why had she been forced to see the horrible things she had seen or live through one of the most difficult times in the history of the world? Why had she been given those kinds of memories, of being forced to live in the Warsaw Ghetto, to watch her family members die off one by one, to hear the news that one of her younger brothers had joined the resistance and been killed? It all felt so unfair to me.

I had a very specific sense that she had met Jesus after her death, and that, somehow, He was holding her, somehow providing her comfort for all of the difficult things she had seen and gone through. And I felt so grateful, you know? I had been blessed with those last few days, and especially those last few minutes. I had been blessed to have that time with her. I wanted to smile and cry and scream and laugh all at the same time.

In the days following the funeral, we sat *shiva* for her, a Jewish tradition where the family of the deceased mourns for a particular amount of time, gathering together and welcoming visitors. The word "shiva" actually means seven, and sitting shiva normally lasts for seven days. We could only stay in California for three, but it was a deep and meaningful time for our family, meeting some of our friends and spending time with each other, sharing old stories and memories of Mother.

There we were, in my brother's living room, all of us sitting on these little boxes — you have to sit on a box when you sit shiva. In mourning after a Jewish funeral, the family isn't allowed to cook, so friends and neighbors bring in food. You cover up all the mirrors in the home because it's all about the deceased.

We spent all that time reminiscing, and because of all we'd been through, we laughed as much as we cried during those days, recalling what a spitfire she had been, how full of life. It really was a beautiful thing, being able to spend time together with my family after we had lost someone who had been such a constant part of our life for so long.

For months after she passed, I would check my phone late at night, only to realize she hadn't left me a voicemail complaining about her day or wondering where I was or telling me she loved me.

"Oh, Mom," I would think to myself in those moments, "I miss you so much."

~ ~ ~ ~ ~

After losing my mom, we just weren't prepared for the incredible amount of sadness that was still headed our way. Only weeks after we buried her, the family was confronted with another heartbreaking situation.

I should start by saying that my daughter Sonya has always wanted children. When she was 18 years old, we performed at Dollywood (as we do every year during the fall), and even though she wasn't married at the time, she was so excited at the thought of someday having children that she bought this little ruffly dress with strawberries on it, a bonnet, and matching bloomers. For some reason, that outfit caught her eye, and she said, "Someday, I'm going to put this outfit on my daughter."

When she and Jimmy got married, they had their first child, a boy, and they named him Ayden. Around his third birthday, she was pregnant again. About three months into the pregnancy, they discovered the baby was a little girl, and Sonya was beside herself. She even did a Facebook post with the strawberry dress in hand, telling the story, revealing that she was having a girl, and rejoicing that her daughter would wear that dress. Everything was going along so well.

Soon after that, my mom fell in California and fractured her hip. We didn't realize at the time how bad it was, or how her condition was worsening. Then came the call, my flight out, and her last days. I remember so specifically Sonya's words during my mother's funeral. She told everyone she was carrying a baby girl and would name the baby after my mom: Ayva Devorah. My mother's name had been Fiegl Devorah, and both the baby's and my mother's names meant Little Bird.

Soon after we returned to Tennessee, a few weeks after Mom passed away, it was time to hit the road again. We performed at Dollywood and then went on to Hiawassee, Georgia, for the Georgia Mountain Fair. I remember that morning clear as anything, when everyone was getting their showers for our afternoon performance and Sonya's voice came out to me.

"Mom?" she said. "Can you come in here for a second?"

She noticed she was bleeding, and we didn't know what to do. It was Sunday, but because Sonya's OBGYN knew she traveled, he had given Sonya his cell phone. She explained to the doctor what was going on.

"Try to stay off of your feet until you get home," the doctor said. Sonya still wanted to sing that day, so we put out a tall stool for her and she did the hour-long show that way. We told the audience she needed to be off her feet for a few days because of her pregnancy. Afterwards, we got back on the bus and made the four-hour trip home. I was on the couch with her the whole time, pampering and encouraging her. We were all so nervous about what might be happening.

We got home around 11 p.m., and Jimmy was waiting to take her into the hospital. They admitted her, and the doctor was going to come in that night to do an ultrasound and have Sonya take some tests. The whole situation felt so heavy, and I found myself crying out to God over and over again to protect the child, protect Sonya, and help everything work out.

When the woman came in to do the ultrasound, I looked over her shoulder at the screen, hoping to see something positive. Anything. Jimmy was sitting beside me holding Sonya's hand. The only thing I thought I could tell was that there wasn't any movement. I couldn't see a heartbeat. I had seen a lot of ultrasounds in my years, and the first thing I always looked for was the tiny beating of the heart. Sometimes, when they turned on the color, you could see the red pulsing quickly. As I stood there looking at the monitor, my heart was pounding because I couldn't see a heartbeat. There was no glimmer of anything beating. I didn't make eye contact with Sonya or Jimmy because I thought the expression on my face would give it away. There was a pit in my stomach, but I had to keep it inside.

Being a mother, I felt the fear of that moment.

We had to wait two hours for the doctor to arrive and come back with the results of that ultrasound. What a long two hours that turned out to be.

I guess it was around two in the morning when the doctor came back into the room and sat down with us, right there beside the bed. I didn't think that was a good sign.

"I'm sorry," the doctor said, "I don't have good news for you."

My breath caught in my throat.

"There is no heartbeat."

We sat there in silence, all of us holding our breath. How could it be true?

"It seems that your baby passed away a few weeks ago."

Sonya was devastated. We all were. It seemed there was no amount of tears we could cry to make it better. What a heavy thing to live through. Making it even more difficult was the fact that Sonya would need to deliver the baby as soon as she was ready. They would induce labor, and she would bear this child, and then we would bury her. Oh, how my heart ached for Sonya and Jimmy! I wished I could do it for her — I really did.

The doctor delivered this horrible news with kindness and patience. "Do you want to go home and get some rest, then come back tomorrow for the labor and delivery, or do you want to stay and induce labor now?" The rest of us left the room so that they could have some time to think it over.

Walking those hospital hallways, I cried out to God again, praying that He would give Sonya strength, praying that they could make it through this. I thought again about that little strawberry dress, how long she had waited for a baby girl, and how loved this child was, even though she would never see this world alive. I thought about what Sonya had said at my mother's funeral, and I cried again, because I had so wanted this little Ayva to walk the world and be a representation of my mom.

But I also wondered if my mom was waiting for Ayva, or perhaps they were already together. Maybe my mother was holding her. I don't know how these things work in heaven, but the idea of my mother holding little Ayva close and rocking her did my heart good.

I felt so numb. Within the span of only ten days, I had lost my mother and now my granddaughter. My own daughter was nearly drowning in pain and disappointment. It felt like our family was being pushed in from all sides.

Sonya and Jimmy decided to have the baby while they were there, without going home first. I totally understood, and we all prayed for Sonya before and during her labor. When little Ayva came into the world, she took our breath away.

There she lay, perfectly formed, with ten fingers and ten toes, only six months along but so beautifully and wonderfully made. One of the nurses came in with a little purple blanket and wrapped her in it carefully. The entire family came in and took turns holding that tiny, precious child. We were all crying. The room felt like holy ground, like something beyond what we could understand was taking place. I held her, wondering about her short life. I had so many questions for God. I guess I'll have to ask when I get to heaven.

Sonya and Jimmy decided to have a funeral for Ayva, and the hospital staff suggested a funeral home in the area that provides free burial service for stillborn children. There is an entire section of the graveyard dedicated to stillborn children, and an 80-year-old woman also associated with the hospital crocheted outfits and donated them for babies like Ayva. It was a beautiful funeral in the midst of a difficult time.

First my mother, and then Ayva. I could only imagine how hard it was for Sonya. It sure was difficult for me, as her mother, because I wanted to do all the hard things for her. I wanted to take that burden off of her. I wanted to take the sadness from her and feel it myself, keep her from all of that pain. But sometimes, as parents, all we can do is walk alongside our children when they are suffering. It's one of the hardest things in life.

I entered a long state of numbness after these two losses. It all seemed too much to believe. Did all of this really happen in the span of a few weeks? Did I really sit with my mother while she died? Did I really stand by while my daughter gave birth to her stillborn daughter? Had we really all walked alongside Ben as he tried to help his family member struggling with addiction? How would Becky's physical and emotional health hold up under these circumstances?

It all felt like our family was under a terrible attack. And it felt very personal, like the enemy knew the things that meant the most to us and attacked those areas of our family relentlessly.

But we still had to sing, every weekend, and in some ways it was the singing that kept me sane, because we had to be strong. I might have slept the days away, spent entire chunks of my life in bed feeling sad, but I couldn't, because we had an audience waiting for us, and I knew there were people in the audience going through things every bit as hard as what we had gone through. I wanted to be there for them, with them. So we sang.

In the singing, I began to remember the promises of God.

There are so many beautiful promises in the Bible, promises that God has made to us and that He will always deliver on. No matter how difficult those times were, I always felt that God was close, that He would save us, that He would be faithful and deliver us from all of our troubles.

Out of that time came deep and meaningful songs. Sonya has always said, "There's no testimony without the test." And it has never been truer than during those days in 2014. Overcoming together as a family drew us even closer together, and we held each other up, reminding each other that God would help us through. We leaned on the Lord and our church families and our close friends.

One of the main reasons we made it through these things was because we did it as a family, and my children are strong people. We knew our roles, and we knew how to step into these tough situations and help each other. But sometimes roles change. Sometimes being a daughter can mean one thing now and a completely different thing later in life.

My roles in life were changing, and there were more tough things on the horizon. But one thing wouldn't change — I was still Lily Fishman Isaacs, going through life wearing my wedding dress and combat boots.

CHAPTER
7

Sometimes, the label of who you are stays the same even as your identity and purpose change. I've been a daughter my entire life, but when I was a baby, that meant one thing, and when I was a teenager, it meant something entirely different. As I got older, and as my mother got older, the role I played as her daughter began to shift.

When my stepfather died in 2006, my mom was 86 years old, and by then, yes, I was still her daughter, but I was also her caretaker. Yet she never let her age stop her! She still climbed into her car almost every day, an old 1980s Buick she parked in the garage under her apartment building. Getting out of that tight space required some serious driving skills, maneuvering out from between cars that were parked in like sardines side by side by side.

But she had done it for 50 years. She took the car and went to the fish market five or six blocks away, stopped by the vegetable store, had lunch, then went home and parked in the underground garage.

At some point in those later years, we hired a helper to be with her at home from around nine in the morning until six at night. Her name was June, and she went along with Mom on these daily trips to the store. Mom would always parallel park, and she was still quite the driver (even if she did occasionally bump the car behind her).

When my Mom parallel parked, she would squeeze into a spot made for a compact car, but hers was a Buick. A big car. A sedan. So she'd back up in the spot and bump the car behind her, then she'd go forward and bump that car. She did this two or three times until she got into the space. Sometimes she even set off the car alarms of the cars on either side! But she didn't care — as long as she parked her car. A bump here and a bump there, but you get it in — that was my mother.

The two of them always had lunch at a little diner right there in New York City, and Mom bought groceries for supper every day. Mom took pride in cooking for her and June. Well, one day the two of them climbed into the car and Mom turned the ignition and began pulling out, but, instead of pushing the brake, she pressed the gas, hitting a parked car in front of her. She caught herself (not quite in time) and quickly put it in reverse, but then backed into the parking garage wall. June jumped out of the car and ran around to get Mom out of the car.

The superintendent of the building came out, and I can only imagine his response, seeing the wrecked cars and Mom's old Buick pressed up against the cement wall. The car required some serious repairs, and once my brother and I found out about it, we knew we had to do something. We decided it was probably time for her to stop driving.

After that accident, I went to New York to talk with her about it and kind of feel out where she was in regards to giving up her driver's license. The accident had scared her quite a bit, and at the end of the day we just had June take over the driving responsibilities, which meant Mom's routine remained pretty much the same. She maintained some of her independence, only it was through June.

That was the first thing that we did that took away her independence. She was 86. I know it hurt her. All those years she took such pride in being independent, and all the years I was growing up, Mom was the only driver until my brother got his license. That was her life, part of her identity, and she was proud of it. Taking that away stripped her of so much of her self-worth. I know it was painful for her, and it really grieved my brother and me to do that. I watched some of her fiery personality dim when she didn't have her license anymore, but I knew it was the right thing to do.

My role as a daughter continued to change quite a bit in those years. Soon after that accident, we talked with her about moving into assisted living. Eventually, we had to force her to do it, but once she was there, she loved it. All those friends and parties! She really fit in well and enjoyed her new community. But again, as a daughter, I had to work with my brother to help my mother navigate this new time in her life. This was nothing like being a teenage daughter or a daughter in elementary school. This meant being a completely different kind of daughter, one who took care of my mother, instead of the other way around.

It was strange, that shifting of the daughter role from being cared for to being the caretaker. My mother had raised me, provided for me, and for many years had been the one I tried to impress, to please. My dad was a good man, but he was so consumed by his own grief, just trying to survive, that he never got very involved in his children's lives. The most important thing to him was to make sure we had plenty of food to eat. So my mother had to be both mother and father. She was the one who came to the school plays and teacher meetings. And now there we were, the roles almost completely switched. My brother and I were looking after her. She was calling me every night, checking in. It felt like she needed me in completely new ways.

Sometimes our roles can change drastically. Often these things happen to us and do not come about by our own choosing. We don't plan the bad diagnoses, the accidents, or the incapacitations. We don't leave our house one day and say, "Today would be a good day to ruin a friendship" or "Today I'm going to get bad news from the doctor."

A few years ago, I didn't set out that day thinking, "Today would be a wonderful day to get into a car accident."

But we can't control everything.

~ ~ ~ ~ ~

In May of 2016, I was cruising down the road, minding my own business, driving to our bus to load up some CDs and retail items before our next trip. I was about a mile from my destination, traveling on a perfectly straight stretch of road, going around 45 mph. That's when a woman driving a white SUV pulled out in front of me from her driveway, out onto the two-lane highway.

It was such a strange thing. I can still picture it all in my mind: the SUV pulling out, realizing it was too late for me to stop, getting closer and closer and bracing myself. She panicked, and instead of pulling out faster, simply stopped. I swerved, but didn't have time to miss her completely, and my car crashed into the passenger side of her SUV. The air bags went off, hitting me hard in the chest.

Those post-accident moments are other-worldly. Maybe you know what I mean. Maybe you know the silence that settles in a doctor's office after you receive the diagnosis you didn't think you'd get. Maybe you have experienced the buzzing in your ears and felt your pulse beating hard after you found out your spouse was having an affair, or the accountant told you the bad news, or insurance informed you they don't cover that.

There we sat, parked in the middle of the road. A guy in a truck stopped traffic and called 9-1-1. Far in the distance, I could hear the sirens wailing. A thin haze of smoke rose from the steering column, so I grabbed my phone from the passenger seat, unbuckled my seatbelt, and jumped out of my car, worried it was going to catch on fire. I rubbed my hands up and down my arms and legs, making sure all of my limbs were attached. I looked around in shock. The cars were both destroyed, and my first thought was that the person in the other car must be dead. She was still in the car, and the man who had stopped came over and helped her out. She was okay. Thank God.

I had the hardest time breathing. The police had arrived, and an officer walked over to my car and helped me sit down. We talked about what had happened. The other woman was limping. They asked me a lot of questions.

"Do you need an ambulance?" one of the officers asked me.

"I don't know," I said. "But I'm having trouble breathing."

I decided to go to the hospital, and the ambulance came, and they administered oxygen, eventually taking me to the emergency room to check me out. I never saw the other woman again.

I called my family, and my son-in-law John and Sonya came. In the ER, they checked me over but didn't see anything major. They did catch a tiny fracture in one of my ribs from the air bag, and they gave me an inhaler and told me to check back with my family doctor in a week or so. A couple days later, I was so sore, and I had a red line that formed an impression from where the seatbelt had caught me as well as where my arm had hit the steering wheel.

A week later, I finally made time to go in and see the family doctor.

"I'd like to do a CT scan," she said, "to check on your heart and lungs." We did, and after the report came in, she called. I was on the bus getting ready for a show.

"Well, the report is back," she told me over the phone. "Two things jumped out at me. Your implant from your breast surgery, the one you had put in after you had cancer? It looks like it has ruptured, so you should get that checked by a breast surgeon."

Because I had a mastectomy due to breast cancer in 1983, I had a breast implant inserted in 1987, and it had lasted all those years.

She paused.

"Is there something else?" I asked.

"You do have a little spot on your right lung."

"A spot?"

"I'm going to refer you to a pulmonary surgeon, just to have it checked out. This isn't anything to worry about, Lily." She knew me. She knew where my mind was going. Every little thing that happened, I went to the worst place. This is a part of my identity that I could probably work on.

I had to schedule a breast surgery to have the implant replaced, and that went well. I made another appointment with a pulmonary surgeon after that to schedule another scan on my lungs, and then I met with the surgeon to discuss the spot.

I was so pleased that the surgery went well, but I still had to deal with the spot, which was terrifying. Any time you're a cancer survivor, that kind of news can take you into a tailspin of fear and anxiety.

"I think it might be scar tissue," he said. "Let's check on you again in six months."

~ ~ ~ ~ ~

These aren't things we orchestrate. These aren't things we plan or ask for or think will ever happen to us. And then they do, and we're left wondering if we can possibly get through it. I felt that way with my back surgery and breast cancer, and later on, divorce and losing my mom, and Sonya losing her daughter. These tough things hit us when we least expect them to. The only thing we can do is put on our combat boots, know who we are, and keep going.

You can get through it.

The human ability to be resilient is amazing, and if you keep going, if you refuse to give up, you will surprise yourself. You will adjust, even if it means rearranging your entire life. I know because I've done it! I've lived alone now for over 20 years, and guess what? I've gotten used to it. I'm independent now, and I don't need a spouse to make a living for me. If you would have asked me to live this life in my 20s, I would have been terrified. This isn't a path I would have chosen for myself, entering the last part of my life on my own. But I'm here now, and I'm thriving.

I have to move past my worry about the worst-case scenario, because guess what? Even if the worst case happens, and sometimes it does, we have to continue believing that God has a purpose for our lives. No matter the interruptions, no matter the surprises, no matter the intrusions.

God has a plan.

~ ~ ~ ~ ~

By the end of the process, I had three CT scans on my lungs, and all three came back looking identical. I sat there in the doctor's office and looked over at him, and he told me it was probably scar tissue that I had in my lungs my entire life. Nothing was growing or changing, so it didn't look like it was anything to be concerned about.

I didn't have lung cancer. Finding that out was a huge relief! But a few years later the diagnosis wouldn't be so reassuring.

CHAPTER
8

About 20 years ago, shortly after our divorce, I had a sharp pain behind my ribs. I stood there for a moment, my hand up to my chest, and I was terrified. Was I having a heart attack? My arm wasn't sore, and I didn't feel faint. It felt too strong to be heartburn, but I couldn't be sure, and the pain kept coming and going in waves, so I called my family doctor and made an appointment for the next day.

The doctor ran me through a battery of tests, including blood work and a chest x-ray, but nothing unusual showed up. They did an EKG to check my heart, but that seemed fine, thankfully. Finally, he thought it might be my esophagus, so we scheduled an appointment with a gastrointestinal doctor, and he scheduled an endoscopy for the following week.

That day, when I woke up from the procedure, the doctor told me I had a condition called Barrett's esophagitis. It's a condition some people live with for their entire lives and don't even know it. I had some precancerous tissue, or dysplasia, that they wanted to biopsy, and it came back benign. Of course, I was concerned since I'd had breast cancer 15 years before that. I didn't like to hear the "c" word.

"Don't worry," my doctor told me. "It's a treatable condition. We'll put you on Prilosec to keep your heartburn at a minimum. We'll need to do an endoscopy every two years, just to keep an eye on things, and if you have any additional dysplasia, we'll go ahead and treat it."

"I don't like hearing the word 'cancer,'" I said.

My doctor gave me a kind smile and nodded. "I understand, Lily, but there's nothing to worry about. We'll keep a close eye on it, and if anything comes up, we'll catch it early. It's a very common condition."

I became very proactive with my health, going in every two years for an endoscopy. They would biopsy any dysplasia, and the tests always came back negative. No cancer. I was just sailing through life, and after years of having these tests done, I barely even thought about my condition anymore apart from the biennial appointments. I did continue with my yearly checkups and mammograms.

Then came 2017.

I had moved to Nashville not too long before then, and I remember thinking that I hadn't received a letter from my doctor to schedule the endoscopy. I called their office.

"Hi," I said. "I just wanted to check in because I think it might be time for me to schedule my endoscopy. I think it's been two years."

"Yes, you're right," they said.

"I need to move my records, because I live in Nashville now." So I found a new doctor at Vanderbilt, and he received my file. An endoscopy was scheduled.

Becky took me to the appointment because they usually put me to sleep with anesthesia to do the test, and after that, I couldn't drive home. I wasn't feeling apprehensive at all. I'd had so many endoscopies by that point that it all felt incredibly normal. But when I woke up from that one in 2017, what the doctor told me changed my life.

"In the endoscopy scope," he said, "I saw a tiny nodule. It was very small, down at the base of your esophagus." He paused, and I felt those old fears rising in me. "I don't think it's anything to worry about, but we cut it out, and we'll biopsy it, only because that's normal procedure."

"Should I be worried?" I asked him. "Because I am."

He smiled. "It doesn't look concerning, Lily. But let's reschedule for three months from now. That way I can repeat the procedure, make sure we got it all, and go from there."

When I left the doctor's office that day, I felt very uncertain. Even though the doctor had told me over and over again not to be concerned, I couldn't help but worry, and those two or three days felt like torture. My mind went crazy with what-ifs. I just could not get the worst-case scenario out of my mind. I tried to be positive, work hard, and stick to my routine, but somewhere in the back of my mind I knew there was a biopsy being analyzed. I was distracted and had to work hard at simply trying to breathe. I know that was normal with the anxiety I was feeling. I tried to be strong and hide my fear because you can't walk around worrying all the time. But every time the phone would ring, my heart started racing. I was a cancer survivor, and I had always wondered if it would come back. I prayed every day that all would be well, that I would not have cancer, and that my esophagus would heal from the recent procedure.

When I received the call from the office, I knew it was serious because it was the doctor's voice. Doctors don't usually call. Usually it's the nurses. I was at home, and when I heard his voice I went into my bedroom and got down on my knees and held my Bible.

Dear Lord, this is not good.

"Lily," he said, "your biopsy has come back. There were malignant cells in the nodule."

Oh, no, I thought. *After all these years.*

Once again, I felt like I was standing at the edge of a cliff.

"I'd like you to continue taking Prilosec. In fact, I'd like you to double your dose for now. Let's repeat this procedure in three months."

Fear consumed me. I prayed every day, for protection, for healing, for life. I didn't want to die. I wondered if this was it. Were these my final months? I felt so helpless and desperate.

But the more I thought about it, and the more I prayed, the more I realized I had no choice: I needed to trust God and trust my doctor. None of it was in my power. I had to release my fear and trust in those whom God had placed in my path. I could do this. I had to put on my combat boots and march right into this.

Those three months crept by. In September, I returned to the doctor's office, extremely nervous. When I woke up from the procedure, the doctor was in my room again.

"Lily, there was a tiny little spot under the nodule. It could very well be scar tissue, but it was very small. We removed it, and we need to biopsy it."

Lord, why is this happening? I just don't understand.

"How does esophageal cancer work?" I asked the doctor. "What if it is cancer in there? Will you try surgery? Chemo? What can I do?"

"There is a procedure called an ablation," he explained carefully. "They can be very effective. We go in where we scoped you and freeze the unhealthy tissue. This causes new tissue to grow, healthy tissue. It's very effective, but there's nothing we can do until your existing redness clears up. That's our plan— hopefully, assuming we got all of it, once your tissue heals from this procedure, we'll go in and do an ablation."

I felt like I was in a fog.

"In the meantime," my doctor said, "let's plan a PET scan. I'd like to make sure your lymph nodes are clear and that nothing has spread."

A PET scan? Checking to make sure the cancer has not spread to my lymph nodes? It all felt like a nightmare. I nodded and left the hospital, but fear was suffocating me. It was an exact reminder of what had happened to me in 1983 when they had found the lump in my breast. The thought of going through that process again was crippling.

As I've said before, I'm a private person, and I wasn't ready to tell the world that I had cancer again. I had a small circle of friends and family at the time, and those are the only ones I told. Many times, when you're in the public eye and share a personal story, everyone wants to come up and tell you their similar story, including ones that didn't end well. "Oh, my Aunt Sally had cancer," someone might say, "and she died a few months later." I just didn't need to hear all of that negativity. I wanted to focus on life and staying positive, so I kept the news to a very small group of trusted people.

I scheduled the PET scan as well as an appointment with another surgeon to get a second opinion. My doctor had told me that esophageal surgery is very drastic and only a last-resort kind of option. They cannot take out a small piece — they have to remove the entire esophagus, because the tissue is so soft, and you can't attach anything to it or stitch it together. After removing the entire esophagus, they would have to pull up the small intestine. It's an entire reworking of the digestive system, and it's only done in the worst cases.

I had to learn more, so I met with the surgeon. This time, I went by myself to Vanderbilt. I had to be strong. I needed to go by myself this time; I knew I did. I had to face my fear head on, just to know that I could. I was so anxious I don't think I ate the entire day before. It's good to have a support team, but sometimes you just have to plow through things. He explained the surgery to me, echoing what my doctor had told me. It's serious. It's invasive. It's not recommended.

I clutched tightly to my purse, which held my Bible.

Lord, help me not to panic, I prayed.

"Doctor," I said to the surgeon, "please tell me. What would you recommend?"

He smiled and shook his head. "I'm sorry, Lily. I can't make a recommendation in this case. You have all the facts. This is a decision you have to make."

I paused.

"If I was your mother or your sister, what would you tell me to do?"

He paused. He looked at me for a moment. "If that was the case," he said hesitantly, "I would tell you to try the ablation, because you have caught it early. But I can't tell you what to do."

Two doctors told me the same thing. My original doctor told me he had never lost a patient to esophageal cancer. It was time to trust the process, to move forward in the path that was laid in front of me.

Lord, I don't want to do this! I can't believe this is happening. But I need you to go with me. I'm standing at the edge of the cliff again.

The first bit of good news arrived with the PET scan — everything came back normal. The cancer had not spread, and all signs pointed at it being contained in a small nodule at the base of my esophagus. That gave me a bit of relief. I started to pray that when the second biopsy came back, it would show that the first had been incorrect, that the spot wasn't malignant.

But that didn't happen. The second biopsy came back and confirmed the first. The cancer cells were malignant. My prayer became that, during my next endoscopy in three months, it would be clear so that the doctor could go ahead with the ablation.

I also brought my holistic doctor on board, wanting to make sure I was covered on all sides. She insisted that I stop eating sugar and dairy, to which I reluctantly agreed.

"Lily, sugar feeds cancer, and dairy causes inflammation. If you will stop eating these things, your body will be in much better condition to deal with this cancer."

I stopped eating sugar and dairy, just like that, and I proceeded to lose 30 pounds, not by choice. Every day when I got on the scale, I was losing another pound, and I know that was because of the change in my diet. Her encouragement gave me a sense of purpose, that there was something I could do to fight this cancer. It was motivating, and I didn't feel so helpless anymore because I was doing something. Now, my diet consists mostly of fresh fruits and meat and rice. No dairy, no sugar (apart from natural sugars in fruit and vegetables). And even up until today, I haven't gone back. I've continued with the same lifestyle of eating.

~ ~ ~ ~ ~

During this time of fear and waiting and uncertainty, I turned to my close friends. Two of them are Pastor Greg Devries and his wife Gretchen.

Greg pastors a church called The Well in Scottsboro, Alabama, where he's been ministering to people for a long time. Our family met him four or five years ago when we sang at his church. He and his wife Gretchen are a beautiful couple, and you'd never know they have 12 children.

Because of this new friendship, Greg and Gretchen joined us on one of our trips to Israel. Through that ten-day trip, we got to know them even better. Greg is a prophetic man of God. He would often pray for me, and in his prayers he would bring up things no one else in the world knew about.

A little after the Israel trip, we started having a prayer service here in Nashville. I think it was my daughter Becky and Alison Krauss's idea. It was on their hearts to do something for those in the music industry, to encourage us and lift us up. Every weekend we performed, giving ourselves to others, and we needed a safe space to pray and be ministered to. These services were private, and we'd pray for one another, keeping everything to ourselves. We would share our needs, and all of our friends would come together and pray.

At the first prayer service, Pastor Greg was there. Other artists came, and it was an amazing time of worship and prayer, so we decided to have it once a month. It became the highlight of every month for me, and as I moved into this space of a new cancer diagnosis, I leaned on those times for peace and comfort. The people at the prayer meetings became my closest friends and confidants, and they were constantly praying for me, encouraging me.

Like I said before, I didn't make a big deal about the cancerous nodule, but my friends at this prayer group knew about it. They laid hands on me and prayed for me, and they became my team that kept me strong, checking in to see how I was doing.

During one of these prayer services leading up to my third endoscopy, I so badly wanted the doctors to be able to do the ablation, but they wouldn't be able to do that unless the area was clear of redness. I wasn't eating sugar or dairy. I was taking my medication. I was praying all the time. I went into the natural healthcare clinic every two weeks. I hoped that this combination would lead to a favorable outcome.

In that prayer service, everyone gathered around me to pray for me. Pastor Greg stopped the prayer and started talking to me.

"Lily, I have to tell you this. While we prayed over you, I saw a vision, and you were standing there wearing a wedding dress with combat boots on."

His words brought tears to my eyes, and before I knew it, I was weeping. It was such a powerful visual for me because somehow God was confirming to me that I am the bride of Christ, and that He's pleased with me. But I'm also in the fight for my life, literally. That's where the combat boots came in.

I've never forgotten that visual. I don't think I ever will.

So many of us are there, aren't we? We're wearing our tuxedo or wedding dress, knowing that Christ is in us and with us, but we also have our combat boots on because we're fighting tough battles against things that want to destroy us or distract us from doing God's work. However, we get dressed for a wedding, it's a symbol, but it reminds me of the symbolism in the Bible of when we put on the armor of God. When you become the Bride of Christ, it's almost inevitable that you're going to be in a battle with the enemy. That's how it's been since the beginning of time. And while there's comfort and peace and gratification in knowing God and having His Spirit with us, there are also battles we have to prepare for. Whether it's health or finances or family issues or loved ones battling addiction and depression — there are so many of us fighting, and the battles can be long, and we grow so weary. I'm honored to be wearing that dress. It's been my lifeline for 50 years. But along with it, I've had to be prepared to lace up those combat boots.

In prayer during the following days, we did a seven-day communion fast. We took communion and prayed the prayer for the bread and the wine, and in our prayers we mentioned the names of all those who had needs. I could feel the power of the prayers being said for me, and I was praying hard for them too. I felt comfort knowing that God was with me, even at the edge of the cliff. I knew I was wearing a wedding dress for a reason — I am the Beloved of God! — so regardless of what happened, I knew that I would be covered.

But I had no choice but to leave it all in the hands of God.

The morning of the procedure, December 19th, I went in to the hospital. Pastor Greg called me and prayed for me, and I received ten or fifteen texts from friends who were praying.

God was in control. Once again, I put on my combat boots.

Here we go, I thought.

~ ~ ~ ~ ~

Going in for that third endoscopy felt like a big deal. If my esoph-agus was clear, they could do the ablation, and that would be our first major step in getting rid of the cancer that was there. The day of the procedure, I could only have liquids. Becky and Sonya took me in to the hospital, and I sat in the waiting room with fifty other people, each with their own concerns and fears and anxieties. I was called back into a holding area. The only things I had on were my underclothes and a prayer cloth that I've worn for the last 35 years. Through the years, I continued adding small cloths with additional scriptures written on them, pinning them all together. It's a reminder, a connection to the prayers I've prayed over my life.

I pinned these onto my underwear. The original prayer cloth was prayed over 36 years ago by a man named Brother Pucket. He was around 80 years old at that point, and after Joe and I sang a song, he told me, "Sister Isaacs, the Lord told me to tell you you'll never have cancer again." He handed me a small piece of red cloth.

So when I got the diagnosis, I thought about the prayer cloth. I questioned it. He had said I'd never have cancer again, and I'd trusted that for 30 years, but there I was. It raised so many questions for me. I don't know how to explain it, but I still wear it every day. To me, it's a symbol of holding onto the promise.

There I was, in that small waiting room, and I pinned those prayers onto my underwear. Then came the loneliness.

I was there in my hospital gown, waiting, as alone as I could be. No one was in the room with me, and all I had with me was what I carried in: my Bible. I thought back over my most recent visit to my holistic doctor, when she had been praying for me. After she finished praying, she looked at me and said, "Lily, while we were praying, I saw this color red turn to pink. I think God is making this red inflamed tis-sue heal to pink." In my own prayers, every day, I would put my hand on my chest and pray, "God, red to pink. Red to pink."

Someone came in and wheeled me to the operating room. The doctor was there, and I looked up at him.

"I hope we'll have good news," I said. "I hope my esophagus is clear and you'll be able to do the ablation today."

He looked at me and said, "That's what we're hoping for."

The anesthesiologist came in and put a mouthpiece in my mouth, and I remember clearly the last thought in my brain as I went under as they told me to breathe calmly.

There was a routine I started after the second test, after my diagnosis. I had it in my brain that when I fell asleep with anesthesia I would take in a big breath and imagine I was taking in as much of the Holy Spirit as I could, and when I breathed out, I imagined the Holy Spirit covering my body with that same breath.

Breathing in. Breathing out.

Breathing in. Breathing out.

Trusting in the Lord.

And then I was asleep.

~ ~ ~ ~ ~

When I think back over my life, the image of the wedding dress and combat boots speaks volumes to me. When I was young, I wasn't even sure if there was a God. I didn't know if I believed in anything. After I came to know the Lord, immediately when I decided to follow Jesus, that's when I put my wedding dress on. I guess it was probably a little smaller then! But all of those things, from the beginning when my family rejected me for believing in Jesus, to when I went through all of my marriage issues, to praying at the altar when I was alone, to the day I gave birth to my son Ben and didn't know if my family would accept him — during all of those difficult times, I had my combat boots on.

During my early Christian life, when I had hepatitis and breast cancer and scoliosis surgery, during every single one of those hard times, I was dressed in my wedding dress, ready to meet the Lord, but I also had my combat boots on. There are some periods of life where it seems like the battles never stop. I think I slept in my combat boots during those years!

After surgery, while I was resting in recovery, I learned that my esophagus had healed enough for him to perform the ablation. My family was there with me, and we cried happy tears, believing that everything would be okay. Knowing that it would be okay, no matter what happened.

In the months and years after that, I had seven more ablations, each time going down an inch further, clearing the way. At this point, I'm going every six months for a basic endoscopy.

I keep thinking over my doctor's words: "I've never lost a patient to esophageal cancer." They echo in my mind, and they stir up hope. I have to trust him, and I have to trust God.

Even better, because of the changes I made to my diet, I feel healthier now than I ever have. I have been strict about how I eat, and often I have to take my own food on the road, but it's worth it for me, because this way of eating has changed my life.

But no matter what happens, I have that image that Pastor Greg gave me. "Lily, I have to tell you this. While we prayed over you, I saw a vision, and you were standing there wearing a wedding dress with combat boots on."

Those words still bring me hope no matter what I'm going through and no matter the outcome of any test or biopsy. That is who I am. That is who I will continue to be. And it brings me a lot of peace.

CHAPTER
9

When I was growing up, there were two things I came to understand at a very early age. First of all, I was Jewish. I couldn't have explained what this meant when I was little, but I definitely understood it. Maybe it was because of the services we went to or the things my parents said. But I knew it. I was Jewish. It was in my blood and was a big part of who I, Lily Fishman, was.

But there was something else, a thing that was hidden under the surface of our lives. I don't remember learning about it all at once, but as I got older, I started to comprehend that something terrible had happened in our family history. Eventually (and I don't know at what exact age I came to understand this), I realized that this terrible thing was called the Holocaust. Again, I didn't know exactly what that meant or precisely how it had impacted my family, but I had this sense of a dark cloud hanging over our timeline.

I came to know and understand that none of my grandparents had survived it. Not knowing the feeling of having a grandparent saddened me. I didn't know what it was like to go to Grandma's house or snuggle up next to Grandpa. I never had that. I learned that very few of my parents' brothers and sisters had survived this Holocaust. It was like a monster in my past, something that had devoured up people and places and years. It was a darkness that scared me, something I didn't want to talk about or ask about, and this was good, because my parents didn't want to talk about it either.

And that's how the years moved along, even as I got older. My mother didn't seem like she wanted to talk about her experience in the Holocaust, and my father absolutely refused to talk about it. In hindsight, I wonder if this had led to his alcoholism. I am sure it had a lot to do with him being who he had become. And I wish I would have asked more questions, especially when I got older. I wish I would have pressed him. Maybe he wouldn't have told me anything. But maybe he would have. I guess I'll never know.

Before my mother died I was able to hear many of her stories, but after she died I felt like a great door had been closed on my past. It felt that I had lost so much through the Holocaust, that so many of my family stories and connections and history had been taken and could never be found again. I mourned this for a long time. But it felt like there was nothing I could do to retrieve those old memories, so eventually I moved on with life.

Then my children and I started traveling back to Israel, and seemingly out of nowhere, the life of my family started coming out into the light.

~ ~ ~ ~ ~

For years, we visited Yad Vashem during our annual Israel trip, the Holocaust Museum in Jerusalem. And all that time, I had no idea that they had a historical archive building, a kind of library with shelves from floor to ceiling, filled with books and video clips and family information about Jewish families who were impacted by the Holocaust. Whether they lived through the Holocaust or were killed in the Nazi death camps and work camps, there is a record there of their existence.

I never knew that I could enter my parents' names into their Hall of Remembrance, not until the last time we visited. So, after that, I made it my mission. During our next trip there, in 2018, I would make that happen. I would do whatever I had to do to make sure my parents were remembered there.

I checked out the application process online, and there was a fairly detailed form to fill out. It required a lot of information, much of which I didn't have or know, but I wanted to complete as much as I could in advance of our trip so that I could potentially meet with the people who ran the historical archives. I so badly wanted to know more about my family, more about my relatives who lived and died during that time. I thought that if I could give them as much information as possible, they might be able to connect me with the rest of the story.

But the application had so many questions, and I knew almost none of the answers. Grandparents' names and dates of birth, for example. I didn't even know the full names of my grandparents, much less their dates of birth, or how many siblings they had, or the names of their parents. Like I said, my parents rarely talked about the Holocaust, and that meant rarely (if ever) mentioning our extended family. My dad was so quiet, submerged under his alcoholism and weariness and depression. My mom was busy dancing with her friends and trying to make a life out of what she had been handed. And in the 1940s, '50s, and '60s, communication wasn't like it is today. You couldn't simply pick up the phone or email a cousin who lived in Europe. When they moved to New York City, when they came over the ocean and walked onto U.S. soil, they were starting over.

I wouldn't say that their family was something they wanted to forget, but I do think they buried those Holocaust years deep, and they didn't want to constantly be thinking about all that they had lost. I knew my father had a brother in Australia. That was pretty much what I knew about my extended family. Honestly. That was it. Besides my brother, his family, and a few cousins scattered around the world, I had no one left besides my children and grandchildren.

I sent an email to someone at the Yad Vashem historical archives to see what I should do about all the empty spaces in my application. I thought my family should be remembered there. After all, both of my parents had survived the Holocaust. But I just didn't have the information. I asked if I could perhaps speak with someone there who might be able to help me get what I needed to complete the forms. But no one called or emailed me back, so I was at a loss.

Our 2018 trip to Israel was quickly approaching, so I collected all the documents I had — my mother's and father's release papers from the war and some old photos I found in a box when I cleaned out Mom's apartment — and I put them in an envelope to take along on the trip. I decided I'd visit the historical archive in person while we were there, and maybe I could find someone who would answer my questions.

But something else was coming together during the lead-up to that 2018 Israel trip, something that would change my family and lead us in an exciting new direction.

~ ~ ~ ~ ~

During the summer of 2018, as we began to make preparations for the trip to Israel, Sonya mentioned that 2018 marked the 70th anniversary of Israel's statehood. Israel became a Jewish nation back in 1948 (finally, a country the Jewish race could call home), and they were celebrating. After World War II, millions of Jews had no place to go back to. They had nothing. Opportunities arose for people to go to family members in other countries for help. In 1948, Israel opened the borders for all Jews to come there and become citizens, living there for the rest of their lives. The Jewish people finally gained a home, one that could not be taken away from them.

One of the girls said, "We should try to do something special while we're there this time. And this will be our fifteenth trip. We would do something special for the land of Israel."

One of them said, "Wouldn't it be cool if we just went and met with some Holocaust survivors there and gave them some money?"

I thought that was a wonderful idea. I had read recently that a lot of Holocaust survivors were lonely, that many had outlived their families and were struggling to make ends meet in their old age.

But how would we even begin to connect with Holocaust survivors in Israel when we were thousands of miles away?

As I thought more about this idea, I remembered that two or three years before, I had met a young man in Nashville, a Jewish man, and he was involved in an organization called Helping Hand Coalition. Their main purpose was to help living Holocaust survivors all around the world. When I first met him, he had asked if we were interested in helping, and we had been, but he moved and we were busy, and we lost contact.

But when my daughters starting talking about this idea, my mind immediately went back to him.

"I'll reach out to David and see if we can get this moving," I said. I called him and left a voicemail. He called me back within an hour.

"I had forgotten we talked!" he said, excited to hear what we were interested in doing.

"Let's get together and talk again," I suggested. "Where do you live?"

"I live in Virginia now. I work at Liberty University."

That stopped me in my tracks.

"Are you kidding me?" I asked. "This weekend we are playing at Liberty! We have a concert lined up this weekend. They are having a Fourth of July celebration and they asked us to sing!"

He laughed. I thought, *These types of coincidences don't just happen, right?*

David and his wife, Rachel, came to our bus early on the day we were scheduled to perform, and all of us went out to lunch, starting to make plans about how we might be able to help Holocaust survivors. He was so helpful and encouraging, telling us we could do what we wanted to do and that his organization would help us in any way we needed.

"You could actually meet some Holocaust survivors while you're there, you know," he said in passing. That got my attention.

"Are you serious?" I asked.

"Oh, yeah. Sure. How many would you like to meet?"

We calculated how much money we thought we'd have, because we wanted to be able to give them gifts, and decided around 150 would be great. After we got home from that concert at Liberty, we started to get excited about the possibilities of this upcoming trip. We would be able to meet Holocaust survivors, just like my parents, and we'd be able to bless them in some way.

It all felt so personal. These survivors were like a ray of light that had somehow come through the darkest time in human history. My parents had been part of that group. We decided we would start up an account where people could donate money for our upcoming Israel trip, and any money we raised, we'd give away. At every concert, we talked briefly about it.

"If you believe in blessing Israel, why not join us? Let's join together as a group of believers in the United States and bless those who survived the Holocaust."

One night during this time, Becky had a vision. God spoke to her spirit and said that we should bless not only the end, but also the beginning and the middle. So we all thought hard about what that meant, how it might impact what we wanted to do. We knew we were going to bless Holocaust survivors, but who would be the beginning and the middle?

It was also during this time that we were booked to sing at the Messiah Conference at Messiah College in Grantham, Pennsylvania. It's a conference where Messianic Jews come from around the world for an entire week, and we were booked to sing there one of the nights. Now, I had met people like me on our travels, Jews who had decided to put their hope and faith in Yeshua, but this conference was unlike anything I had ever experienced. There were 2,000 of us there, Messianic Jews, and it was one of the most exciting times of my life.

During the day, we got to meet so many people. We had lunch and talked with everyone we could, and it felt like I had come home. I can't explain it any other way than that. I had finally found my long-lost community. There we were, in the middle of this huge crowd of people, and everyone had these Jewish sayings and mannerisms and even looked and acted like I did. Honestly. It felt surreal and was probably one of the most exciting times of my life.

It was at that event where we met people who worked with the Joseph Project, whose sole mission was to go in and support orphanages in Israel. They blessed people whether or not they were Messianic. And that's when it clicked for us — the beginning. These orphans were "the beginning" Becky had encountered in her vision. God put His stamp of approval on it, and we knew we wanted to support the Joseph Project along with the Holocaust survivors.

We sang, and the concert went well, but it was part of the larger event going on that night. Later on, one of the main speakers asked all of the other speakers and entertainers to come back up on the stage.

"You are all on the road most of the year, speaking to masses of people, millions of people, and we'd like to cover you in prayer," the speaker said. So we all moved in close together. I guess there were about 15 of us on the stage — ministers and staff and everyone started praying over each other.

Right in the middle of this beautiful moment, Rabbi Michael Wolf, an old friend of mine from Cincinnati and one of the main speakers at the conference, moved over to where our family stood. He is the rabbi of the Beth Messiah Synagogue, and he started speaking loudly to us, putting one of his hands on Levi's shoulder and the other hand on mine. Levi is Becky's son, my first grandchild, the next generation. We moved in closer to him until we had surrounded him.

"This family," he said, "has a special anointing. God is going to take you to new places, and out of the ashes will come gifts of love and blessings to people who have suffered."

Oh my goodness.

We cried. Levi got down on his knees and bawled like a baby. It was a confirmation from God that we were supposed to do this thing we had set out to do, and what a confirmation it was. We felt so good about it.

Those early weeks were really the foundation for what we decided to do, and Rabbi Wolf's word gave us the confidence we needed to move forward in a new way. We decided to start a nonprofit organization to honor my parents and all of the Holocaust survivors in the world. My daughters came up with the name, "Fishman Isaacs Israel Initiative." It was very exciting to do this, because this way people could get a receipt for their donations, and we'd be able to disburse the funds to organizations in Israel.

We told even more people about it at our concerts and started a page on our website. Money was trickling in, some here, some there. We had set our initial goal at $25,000, thinking it would be amazing if we could raise that much in such a short time, but before we knew it, we had exceeded our initial goal and raised it to $50,000.

Sonya and Jimmy have a beautiful family chapel beside their house, a gorgeous little place that holds around 70 people. A few years ago, Jimmy wanted to surprise Sonya, because they had always talked about having a small chapel somewhere on the property where they live. Within a few months, he built this beautiful chapel on the property without her knowing it. Occasionally we would get together there as a family and pray as well.

Sonya said, "Why don't we have an online performance and invite some of our friends in music to come to the chapel and perform? We'll sell the seats for big donations, have a dinner, air this little concert, and all the money we raise can go towards the Israel initiative?"

What a wonderful idea. We planned it for late September and arranged for it to air live so people could donate while it was going on. Sonya reached out to our friends in country music, and everyone was so generous. Dolly Parton and Reba McEntire were both busy on that date, but they donated generously towards the cause. Vince Gill and Amy Grant came. Ricky Skaggs and his wife, Sharon, attended. Karen Peck and Connie Smith came. We put together an entire list of great performers, and even though it rained all night, the dinner was beautiful, and the concert went so well, lasting an hour or so.

I sat there in that chapel, listening to the incredible singers, and I thought about how much my mother would have enjoyed that. She loved performances. She loved listening to people sing. I imagined her there beside me, a smile on her face, looking over at me every so often. I wished she could have been there. I wished I could have told her who each of the performers was, how we knew them, how wonderful they were. I know she wouldn't have understood the church experience or perhaps the gospel songs, but I believe she would have been proud of our reason for doing it.

And during the whole concert, people kept giving money online. It was amazing. Eventually we raised over $80,000, but at the time we started the process of deciding how much to donate and to whom, we had raised around $60,000. We decided to give $20,000 to orphanages, $20,000 to Israeli soldiers (the middle), and $20,000 to Holocaust survivors. We just wanted to bless them. Any leftover money that came in (and it did continue to come in), we would carry over to our next trip.

~ ~ ~ ~ ~

My heart was full. Excitement was in the air. Our vision was finally coming true, with the help of our host company Inspiration Tours and tour director Joel James.

We met our first group of Holocaust survivors in Tiberius. We stayed at the Gai Beach Hotel there, and it had an outdoor dining area with a small stage, and with the help of our friends at Helping Hand Coalition, we were able to invite 25 Holocaust survivors to join us for a meal and short concert. There were 180 people on the tour with us from the States, and we had reserved seats for the 25 survivors.

When the bus arrived, my family along with Karen Peck and her family were waiting in the lobby. As our guests got off the bus, we embraced and welcomed them. They were all dressed up, with most of the men in suits and the women in nice dresses. It was so heartwarming to see how much they appreciated what we were doing. Each of us took an arm with one of them, and we made our way towards the outdoor dining area.

From the moment we came into view, all 180 people traveling with us were waiting, and they surprised us and our guests by honoring the Holocaust survivors with a standing ovation, and the crowd continued applauding until the survivors took their seats. I felt like I couldn't take a deep breath, I was so emotional. They were deeply honored, and I could so easily picture my mother and my father among them. My parents would have been completely opposite in their reactions. My father would have been shy and withdrawn, trying not to look up to let people see the tears in his eyes; however, my mother would have been dancing and raising her arms, celebrating the fact that she was getting applause.

How I wished they would have been there!

The men kissed our hands, and the women kept giving us hugs. I think the event made them feel important, helped them to remember that their lives mattered, what they had been through mattered.

And all along, I felt like I was honoring my family — my own parents as well as their brothers and sisters and parents and cousins and aunts and uncles who had all been killed in the work camps and the death camps, the ghettos and the streets. The ongoing applause was breathtaking.

We all sat at our places, and we had hired an interpreter because most of our special guests only spoke Russian or Hebrew. The interpreter went from table to table, facilitating conversations and introducing people. A lot of them had iPhones and were showing us pictures of their children and grandchildren. We walked around and helped them get their food. It was all so touching and sweet.

Eventually, we took the stage and sang three Hebrew songs, asking them to sing along with us, and they did. They laughed and sang with huge smiles on their faces. Then I told my own story, and the stories of my parents, through the interpreter. I wanted them to feel the connection. I wanted them to get to know my mom and dad. They loved it, and they gave me a huge round of applause when I finished.

Finally, three of them got up and told their story. Many of them were children in the concentration camps or ghettos spread out across Europe. But even though they had been children, they had been old enough to remember what had happened. It was so moving, and we sat there enthralled. You could have heard a pin drop. And at the end of it all, we gave each of them a $100 gift card. They were completely astounded, some of them staring at the card as if it had magically appeared in their hands.

When we walked them to their bus, we were all so full of joy and happiness. I knew, in that moment, that I wanted to keep doing this, to keep blessing these people who had been through so much.

The trip continued, and when we arrived in Jerusalem, we had made arrangements through the Joseph Project to visit the Neve Michael. This orphanage was started by Holocaust survivors and their children. One of the leaders of the orphanage met us there, along with the manager of the home — her name was Hava. She was a Jewish New Yorker who had migrated to Israel in the 1960s, and she looked like a hippie! In other words, she was my kindred spirit, and we immediately clicked. We walked together all day, holding hands and chatting — it was like we had known each other our entire lives.

The children at the home were there because their parents had died or because they were escaping abusive situations. Hava walked us around the grounds, and we saw that there were certain areas for sleeping, certain areas for school, and even places where the children received counseling. They served children between the ages of two and sixteen, and there were eight or ten families who lived on the grounds in their own homes so that when the 16-year-olds aged out, they could move in with one of those families instead of being released into a foster home or having to fend for themselves. This way, they could experience home and family life for two years before they turned 18 and had to join the army.

We were able to spend some time with 12 of the children, singing to them and hearing them sing for us. They had three songs, and then a boy got up and played the flute and recited a poem. At the end of our time together, we gave them a check for $20,000, along with gifts that our people on the tour had brought with them. It was amazing.

We were there during Hanukkah, and all the people on tour had brought gifts with them in their suitcases. So not only did we give them money, but the staff was also able to pass out the goodies we brought with us.

Later in the trip, we hosted an event in Jerusalem at a place called The Pavilion that a friend rented for us. It was gorgeous, and that's where we did our main concert of the trip. We brought in 150 Holocaust survivors and 75 Israeli soldiers for the event, feeding them dinner beforehand and then inviting them to the concert. At the end of the night, once again we were able to hand out gift cards to all of them.

We spread around all the money we had collected, from the beginning (the orphanage) to the middle (the Israeli soldiers) to the end (the Holocaust survivors). We gave the soldiers a gift voucher for Hanukkah, and we also supported an organization that helped lone soldiers who were away from their families during the holidays.

If you're an Israeli citizen, you have to serve two years in the service when you turn 18, boys and girls alike. These teenagers are away from their families for two years, except for a short leave every now and then. We wanted to bring them some joy and holiday spirit during their time of service, and they were very thankful. It was one of the most fulfilling things I've ever been part of.

The trip flew by, and before I knew it, we had gotten to the last day of our journey. We had sung in some of the most unbelievable places, visited with new friends, and been on all the tours that we've done so many times but they still amaze us. We finally got to day eleven of our trip. On day twelve, our final day, we were planning on visiting Yad Vashem, the Holocaust museum, with the group.

But that morning at breakfast, I got a call.

CHAPTER
10

After not hearing back from anyone at Yad Vashem, I wasn't sure how I was going to pull off entering my parents' names in the Hall of Remembrance. No one had reached out to me to help. I was worried and a little discouraged about it.

But the day before our group's trip to Yad Vashem, I got a phone call.

"Is this Lily Isaacs?" she asked.

It was one of the ladies from the historical archives. She introduced herself and kindly apologized for not getting in touch with me sooner.

"I only now saw your email," she explained. "Are you still in Israel?"

"Yes!" I said. "We're coming to Yad Vashem tomorrow."

We agreed on a time to meet. I couldn't wait. What were the chances that she would call me the day before I was going to be there, that she would find my message and decide to call me on that very day? I knew God was directing me. I couldn't wait to see what I might learn about my family and my heritage.

The tour guide set aside some time for my meeting to take place, and while they showed the rest of the group around, my family and I went to meet Oxana, the woman I had spoken with on the phone the day before. She came out and we all introduced ourselves, then we followed her into her office and I told her my family's entire story, starting with what I knew and then bringing her up to the present. She was fascinated.

"I can help you, Lily," she said. "I know I can. Let's start with the information that you have." We went through the documents I had and the dates that I knew, and even though it seemed like such a small amount of information, she was confident they would find out more. This made me so excited. I could hardly imagine what it would be like to learn more about my family, my history, my identity.

We always do a service there with our tour groups, outside the building that holds the ashes recovered from crematoriums from every concentration camp. And above where they buried the ashes is a tombstone or marker that has the name of the specific concentration camp. Standing there was overwhelming. I tear up just thinking about it.

But in 2018, our group had been split into two parts because we had four buses with us and so many people. We had already done one of the services, and the second one was scheduled for after our meeting with Oxana. We asked her if she wanted to join us, just to listen in and learn more about us and what we did. She graciously accepted.

Sonya began the service singing a song she had co-written with a friend called "Train to Hell," a song about the Holocaust, and it's a real tear-jerker. Every single time she sings it, I get emotional. After that, I told my story and the story of my family, as much as I knew. Then we prayed with the group.

Oxana stood there and listened through the entire service, and afterwards she came up to us.

"Your family," she said. "My goodness, what a story. Do you travel?"

Do we travel? That made me smile.

"Yes," I said. "We play music. We travel all around the world, and I share our story wherever I go."

"I'm going to help you," she said. "Let me see what I can come up with, and I'll be in touch."

She had seen our hearts, witnessed how much we cared about the history of the Jewish people. Our people. Connecting with her was such a lovely blessing, and I could tell that she really, truly wanted to help.

I left Israel feeling excited and encouraged about what we might find out about my mom and dad, my grandparents and aunts and uncles and cousins. I sent her another email with more photos and video clips of us singing, along with the video of my mother sharing her story.

"Lily, this is incredible!" she emailed back.

The first thing I thought when we returned home from Israel was that I had to tell my brother about what I was trying to do. The two of us don't always see eye-to-eye on everything — I don't think he understands why I have become a Christian. My parents were never very happy about that, and I don't think he has ever been happy about it either. So I was a little nervous about telling him. I didn't want him to be upset with me, that I had gone ahead and listed our parents in the archives without including him.

"We had a great trip," I told him on the phone the day after we got back. "But I want to tell you that I did start the process to enter their names into the Hall of Remembrance. I really want to honor them."

He was completely on board with it.

"Do you know anyone in the family who might know more information about them?" I asked him. "I just don't have all the information I need, like the names and birthdates of our grandparents or any of their other children."

"Oh, definitely. You should talk to our cousins in Australia. I think at least one of them is very interested in genealogy."

I didn't know them, and so they had completely slipped my mind, but my father's brother Samuel was the only other family member who had survived the Holocaust.

"Don't you remember when Uncle Samuel came to visit us in New York?" my brother asked.

"No," I replied. "I think I was married by then, living in Ohio."

"Oh, yes, that's right. That was the first time our father had seen his brother in 30 years. I connected with his sons. In fact, now that you mention it, I did stay in touch with our cousin Zev for a few years. I kind of remember him mentioning something about a distant cousin who had put together a family tree."

"What? I had no idea!" I exclaimed. "Can you give me Zev's email? This information would be so helpful."

He sent me my cousin's email address, and I sent Zev an email right away, introducing myself, letting him know what I was doing with the application to have my parents remembered in the Hall of Remembrance at Yad Vashem. I asked if he had any more information about our family. When I hit send, I hoped I would hear back.

Fifteen minutes later, I received a call from Australia! I'm not even kidding you. Within 15 minutes, I was on the telephone with my long-lost cousin. He had received my email and couldn't wait to talk.

"Oh, Lily, I've been wanting to talk to you for a long time," he said. "We're cousins, and we don't even know each other!"

"I know, I've been wanting to connect with you too," I said. Just hearing his voice brought tears to my eyes. We shared the same blood, the same DNA, the same history. His parents had been through the same things my own parents had been through, and he had the same questions and uncertainties about his past, his identity, and where he came from.

As we talked, he told me that he had been in Israel only three weeks before we had been there with our group, and he had done the same thing that I had done, entering his own parents' information into the Hall of Remembrance.

Wow! We couldn't believe we had done it so close together.

"Zev," I said, "My brother said you have some information that might be helpful, but I have so many gaps in the story. Mom used to share a little bit about what she had been through, but Dad was so quiet about it."

"My dad was quiet, too," he said. "It makes me so sad to think about how he lived his whole life with that experience inside of him."

We sat there for a moment in the silence, thinking of our quiet fathers and all that they had never told us. I wondered what it was like when they had seen each other all those years ago in New York and wished terribly that I had been there. What had they seen in each other's eyes? What old stories rose up in between them like ghosts? What unsaid things did they understand about each other, just because they were brothers and had lived through the Holocaust?

"Let me send you the research our distant cousin did with the Fishman name," Zev said.

"Thank you so much, Zev. What a blessing."

After I hung up, I couldn't believe how much hope the conversation had given me. The stories of my ancestors were such a huge part of my identity, and I could feel myself getting closer to a breakthrough. I couldn't imagine what it would be like to actually know more about my parents and their families.

The next day, Zev sent me all kinds of documents, along with some notes.

"Look on this page," he wrote. "That's your father's name. Our fathers were actually half-brothers." I thought I had heard that at some point, but I could never be sure. Now there was proof. One mystery became tangible fact.

At the top of one of the other pages were the names of my grandparents. At the top of another page were the names of my great-grandparents. It said when they were born. My great-grandmother died in 1941, and then my great-grandfather died soon after, although a date wasn't listed.

My grandmother was born in 1877 and died in 1916 from typhus. My grandparents had four children together, and after my grandmother died, he remarried my grandmother's first cousin and had two more children, both boys. One of those boys was my cousin Zev's father.

Looking down at the list of my father's full family, there was name after name: Uszar born...Hendl born...Pearl born...all of these siblings and their spouses, their birth dates listed in black and white. Shortly after their dates of birth were their dates of death, and all of them had died in Treblinka. Every single one except for my father and his two half-brothers, Samuel and Meyer (those two are listed on a separate page because they had a different mother). What a horror story, how an entire family was extinguished in that place of terror and death. It made me shudder. And it made me sad. And it made me angry. What right had they to kill my family, who had never done anything to them? For several days, I found it hard to get over the tragedy of it all.

Further down the paperwork, it showed the date of when my father married my mother, and her birthday, and underneath that it showed my brother and me, the date that Joe and I were married, and the birth of my three children. Incredible. That was as far as it went.

There I was, situated in the world, not simply a point in history but connected back and back and back, to all of my Jewish ancestors who came before me. It wasn't just my parents and me; my story went back much further, with grandparents and great-grandparents. And there was tragedy there that had shaped us, horrific things that had killed off nearly an entire generation. But there was also love and hope and new things, and I could finally see my part in it.

~ ~ ~ ~ ~

For several weeks after this revelation, I felt a lot of guilt, and it nagged at me from several different angles.

I felt guilt about the thoughts I'd had towards my father for so many years, how frustrated and ashamed I had been when it came to him, how hard I had been on him. I had always wondered why he wouldn't just wake up, live a happier life, or make better decisions. I wasn't as compassionate towards him as I would have been if I had only known more about his past. I had been a teenager, angry at the many ways my father had embarrassed me with his drunkenness. He was my father, but I didn't really know him.

But now I looked at the world he had lived in, the way he had lost his parents and siblings. It was no wonder he had been an alcoholic. He had lost nearly everyone he loved in Treblinka.

Somehow, even when I was young, I knew he was hurting, but I had never made the effort to break through his barriers. Maybe he wouldn't have responded, maybe he wouldn't have answered my questions, even if I asked them, but I still wish I had tried. And what if he

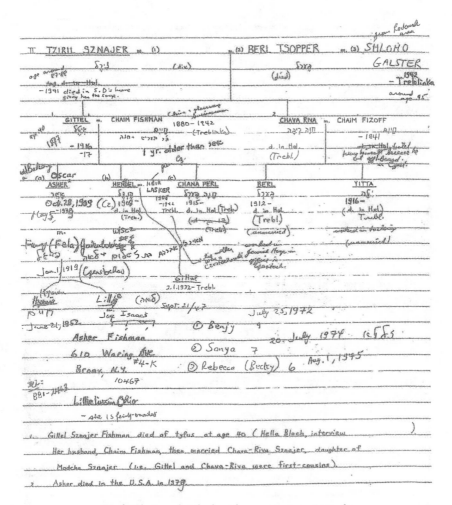

My family tree, sketched out by my cousin in Australia.

had? What stories would I have heard? What facts about my aunts and uncles? What little anecdotes about my grandparents?

I feel guilty that I never asked those questions. It still puts a lonely feeling in my heart because I feel like I was robbed of so much. The more I find out, the more I realize I lost—lost family members, lost stories, lost memories, lost potential.

But more than the guilt, more than the regret, I now feel a huge sense of excitement. It's like finding a treasure, and it's something I can now pass on to my children and grandchildren. I want them to

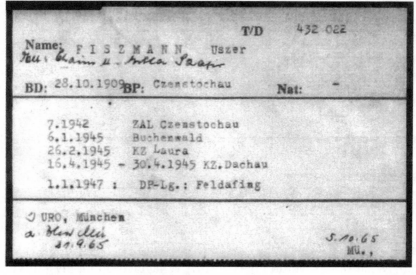

The cards used to track my parents' movements through the Nazi system of concentration camps. Mother's is at the top.

see this, to know it, to realize what their great-grandparents, and their great-great-grandparents went through only 80 years ago. We nearly lost this family history, but now I don't want it to die with me. This legacy has to be told. It will help them find their own identity someday.

Later on, I discovered that the reason my father had not been killed in Treblinka was that he had never even been there. Oxana is still digging up new information, and I get emails from her fairly regularly with revelations about my family. She sends me physical copies when she can, but most of them are written in German, so I need help reading them. One of these documents said my father was in a Czenstachova ghetto for quite some time, eventually ending up in Buchenwald toward the end of the war, from around 1944 to 1945. From there he went to another camp, and he was eventually liberated from Dachau.

Dachau! The infamous place that started as a prison for political dissidents and eventually turned into a death camp. Jews were held there along with artists, intellectuals, and the physically and mentally handicapped. They were given jobs, used as slave labor to create weapons for Germany's war machine. Thousands died there from malnutrition, disease, or simply being executed on the spot.[1] There were over 31,000 registered deaths at the camp, but over 200,000 were registered there as prisoners.

In my father's records, he was only in Dachau for two weeks. Oddly enough, my mother wound up in Dachau the same two weeks. They didn't even know each other yet. Why were they sent there for such a short time period?

Oxana said Hitler found out that the war was coming to an end, and he wanted to destroy all of the evidence as quickly as possible. Dachau had more gas chambers than any other camp in the country. Hitler was gathering as many Jews as he could for the final kill.

Yet, somehow, my father and mother survived.

I know now what I have to do next. I have a new desire burning in me. I have to go to Poland. My cousin was able to give me the address where my family lived. I have to go there, stand on those sidewalks, visit the ghetto where my grandfather lived, search the Czenstachova archives. I have to find out more.

~ ~ ~ ~ ~

---

1. https://www.history.com/topics/world-war-ii/dachau.

The year 2020 started off on a promising note. At the beginning of March, we received an email from the Gospel Music Association (otherwise known as the GMA and the giver of the prestigious Dove Awards) telling us that The Isaacs would be inducted into the Gospel Music Hall of Fame! I almost couldn't believe it; it was one of the biggest honors we'd ever received. The GMA covers so many musical genres: country gospel, southern gospel, bluegrass gospel, contemporary gospel, black gospel, and more.

We were so excited, and we began planning for the awards show in May. They asked us if we could find some artists to sing a song in our honor, plus we needed to come up with some old photos to share. Eventually we received confirmation from our friends and musicians Ricky Skaggs, Natalie Grant, and Vince Gill. Even Terry Bradshaw agreed to be part of the presentation.

As we were planning for this incredible honor, we were also finalizing our trip to Israel and Poland. We wanted to do the same thing we had done the year before, taking along money for Holocaust survivors, children, and Israeli soldiers. We had even started raising money for that trip through the Fishman Isaacs Israel Initiative, and who knows how much we could have raised this time around? Who knows how many people we could have blessed?

We had the idea to include a few days in Poland on our trip so that we could explore the place where my parents both grew up, visit the ghetto where they were held, see the Treblinka concentration camp, and walk the streets where they had lived their lives before the German invasion.

But with the year 2020 came Covid-19, a global pandemic, and all of our plans were for nothing. The trip would have to be canceled. Our induction into the GMA Hall of Fame would be pushed back to May 2021.

I recently found out that there are 5,000 Holocaust survivors left in Poland. My heart is there with them. Maybe someday we can set up a dinner and a concert for them. Who knows? But I do know I want to go to Poland. Breathe the air my parents breathed. I want to feel that ground under my feet.

I'm finding my family, you know? I'm rediscovering my history and, with it, my identity.

This is who I am.

Lily Fishman Isaacs.

And I'm still wearing my combat boots and my wedding dress. I'm grateful for the wedding dress. The laces of my boots are worn. And just when I'm getting comfortable and begin to loosen them, thinking I can take off those combat boots for a moment, something else comes along and I have to tighten them up again. The leather is getting worn on those old boots. It's wearing down. Those boots have served their purpose in many ways. I don't know that I've ever taken them off! I think I sleep in them. But someday I'll take them off, and what a feeling that will be! Not fighting all the time. Not feeling so vulnerable.

What gives me hope is that I know I don't have to do it alone. If I'm the bride of Christ, then I'm the most important thing on His mind. I know He's not going to leave me; He's not going to forsake me. I'm His child. I'm His bride. I'm who He's coming after.

And I know I'll never be alone.

EPILOGUE

O riginally, this was going to be the chapter where I tell you about my first ever trip to Poland, a place we were going to visit on our way home from our next Israel trip. This is where I would tell you how it felt to walk the streets my parents and grandparents walked, breathe that European air, and even see the houses where they lived, the place where they were married, the cemeteries where they are buried. I started this book two years ago and even held off on finishing it until after the trip, because this would be such an important chapter of my story, a time when everything came full circle.

Then came Covid-19.

Our trip was canceled.

Things have changed.

But I still go there all the time in my mind. Sometimes it's when I'm daydreaming about Mom, thinking about her going to the mailbox or putting red lipstick on. Sometimes it's when I'm thinking about Dad sitting at the table reading his newspaper. Sometimes it's when I'm emailing with my cousins.

This is how I imagine traveling to Poland will feel like, someday, in better times.

~ ~ ~ ~ ~

In my imagination, we are descending in a plane, getting ready to land in Warsaw, Poland. The flight from Tel Aviv went smoothly, and after six hours in the air we are equally tired and excited. I look around the huge jet and see my entire family surrounding me. It fills me with a nervous anticipation that is hard to describe.

But I also feel a heaviness, an emptiness, and I actually tear up when the landing gear screeches down on the runway.

After all these years, my feet will walk on Polish soil.

My family and I exchange nervous glances. My youngest grandchildren, Evya and Gatlyn, have very little idea about what's going on. Ayden has heard me tell my story, and he understands a little bit. But all of my grown grandchildren are with me as well — Levi, Jacob, Cameron, Dillon, Kyra, and Jakobi. Their parents are all here, too — Ben and Mindy, Sonya and Jimmy, and Becky and John.

This is a dream come true.

We walk off the plane and collect our luggage and head toward the tour bus we've rented for the trip. The city feels more modern than I expected. Business men and women, dressed in suits, walk quickly from here to there. Everyone's lives look normal and busy, just like they do in America. I stop for a second before walking onto the bus, and tears gather in my eyes. My heart flutters. It might sound silly, but it's almost as if I can feel the presence of my grandparents, my aunts and uncles, my mother and father.

We are in Warsaw. We actually did it.

Because it's late in the afternoon, the first thing we do is head for the hotel. I wonder what was in this part of the city 80 years ago. Houses? Apartments? Were there horses and buggies in the streets? Maybe there were protestors warning about the approach of communism. I can almost see the mothers holding their babies, the fathers walking with their young sons behind them, carrying groceries home.

After a good night's sleep, our first stop is the Warsaw ghetto, where Jews were kept in a kind of holding camp before being sent off to concentration camps throughout Germany and the rest of Europe. My parents told me that when they were sent off to the ghetto, at first they thought they were being taken somewhere to work, and that they would return home. But they never saw their homes again. Millions lost their lives.

While my family did not grow up in Warsaw, a few of them did end up in the Warsaw ghetto. I am so emotional I have to compose myself in order to even look at everything the guide shows us.

The next day, we board the bus for a three-hour drive to Czestochowa, the town where my mother and father were born, where my grandparents were born. I'm not sure how far back my family's roots are in that small town, but someday I want to find out.

My first cousins in Australia brought my aunt to Czestochowa a few years before they died, and they shared the information with me. So we ask the bus driver to try to park near where that street would have been. We all stand there and start to tell stories about my father, how he would tease my children by giving them only one peanut at a time, sometimes hiding them and making the children find the peanut, how he worked so hard, how he always came home drinking.

And I begin to weep uncontrollably.

While my father was alive, I never knew he had lost everyone in his family except one brother. He never talked about his family. All I knew was that they had died in the war. I couldn't understand when I was young. I was just a teenager when I finally understood my father's battle with alcohol, and because he embarrassed me, I was upset with him.

But today, I cry out loud.

If only I would have known, I would have put my arms around his neck and loved him, even more than I already did. I would have told him how much I cared.

As I stand here on his street, I imagine them in their little one-room apartment, all of them together, perhaps celebrating Shabbat dinner, or perhaps the Passover Seder. Maybe he was fighting with his brothers and annoying his sisters. Just a normal little pre-World War II family.

My father, Uszer Fiszman, was born on October 30, 1909, to two parents who had regular lives. He had five siblings at home. His father worked hard as a farmer and a tailor. My father was the oldest and sometimes had to go with his father to work, even on days when he didn't want to … or maybe the house was so crowded he enjoyed getting out, spending time with his father without everyone else around. School was not a priority in those days, and he only attended through the fifth grade. But he was so smart, very intelligent, and had beautiful handwriting.

His grandfather, my great-grandfather, was a rabbi, but I don't know how religious his father and mother were. At some point during his early years, my father's mother Gietel died from typhus at the age of 40. Soon after that, my grandfather met his deceased wife's cousin and they married. I wonder if my father grieved the death of his young mother. I wonder if he felt responsible for the rest of the children. His father and stepmother went on to have two sons named Shulem and Meyer.

How frightened everyone must have been as the war drew closer. They only heard rumors. There were no news outlets, no televisions. And then, one day, the Nazis showed up.

I imagine my father waking up early, running an errand that requires him to take his little brother along with him. They're told over loudspeakers that everyone must go out into the street, and my father somehow loses track of his family. Days later, he's unloaded from a truck. They take all of his belongings and give him clothes to wear — striped work clothes bearing the gold star of David.

My father is taken, along with his little brother Shulem, into a glass factory, separated from everyone else. They've lost their other brother, Meyer. They're taught how to blow glass, and that's where they work for a long time. At night, they ask questions about their missing family, trying to find out where they were taken, what might have happened to them. During the day, whenever he sees a stranger, he asks them about his family. He tells himself they were probably released, sent home.

He dreads to think of the worst, but they hear rumors. After working for this soldier for a few months, they are loaded into the train to hell, and the tracks lead to Buchenwald. The daily meals become smaller and smaller. Eventually, they receive one piece of bread each day, along with a little bit of soup and a cup of water. He loses track of his little brother. They are separated, and he is nowhere to be found.

There were rumors that the war was ending when he was transferred to Dachau. This I know. And he was there for only two weeks when the gates were opened and they were set free. What a day that was! After two years of prison, the freedom of the sky looked so big he couldn't grasp it. What should he do? Where would he go?

He ended up in a kind of refugee camp. There were doctors and nurses there, and he was given food, a blanket, and pillow. The people were kind. He managed to reconnect with his brother Shulem, and together they found one of his other brothers, Meyer. He looked sick, and he didn't survive for very long. He had eaten too much food when he was released, and his shrunken stomach couldn't handle it.

My father found a neighbor who told him what had happened to the rest of his family — they were taken into Treblinka. That's when he knew. They were dead. No one survived the death camp of Treblinka. For years after that, my father had nightmares of the death camp, his whole family stripped naked, heads shaved, skeletons walking into the gas chamber, holding onto each other.

One question I've always had in my mind was, after the people were stripped naked, why did they have their hair shaved off of their entire bodies? Why do this to men, women, and children, only a few steps from the gas chamber?

This question gnawed at me like a cancer. The thought of it broke me. There were all of my extended family, all of my father's family, walking into a gas chamber, stark naked, without a hair on their bodies. It made no sense to me. No one would have seen them, so they weren't being shamed. Was it just to degrade them, to dehumanize them or make them feel more vulnerable just moments from their death?

I did some research on this question, and the findings have haunted me ever since. The Nazis used cyanide gas in the chambers, and cyanide sticks to clothing and hair. So when all of the dead corpses had to be moved out of the gas chambers to be put into the incinerators, where they were burned to ash, the Nazis didn't want their own people to be infected with any traces of cyanide.

The Nazis removed their prisoners' clothing and shaved off all their hair just to protect themselves.

The crying.

The screaming.

The group of them clinging to one another, skeletons falling down around them, his sisters holding onto each other. How long did it take them to die? My father heard that sometimes people survived for days in the chambers if the gas didn't work right. But they kept the doors locked until they knew everyone had died.

What a thought. His baby brothers. His father. All of them.

Then their bodies were burned to ash, and the ash was disposed of like garbage.

My father was taken to Feldafing, Germany, to another refugee camp, where he met a beautiful young woman in her early 20s, a redhead with blue eyes named Fiegel Jackabovitz. He fell in love. They got married.

And I was born.

~ ~ ~ ~ ~

So many memories. So many questions.

My family and I hold each other and cry. But I had to do this. I had to stand on that street, close my eyes, and feel my father's presence. Eventually we move along the street to where my mother grew up. We try to find the exact street, but we're not successful, so we wander around in the general area, and then I can see her in my mind.

By the time my grandfather passed away, the older siblings had gotten married and moved away, but my mother was still at home, the most responsible one of the bunch. She had a sister crippled by polio, and my mother sometimes told me stories of bathing her, taking care of her when her own mother was away or working as a seamstress out of their home.

My mom and dad grew up in the same town, but they never knew each other until after the war. I imagine my mother in her home, sewing something for her mother as people come in and out of the house, customers and friends, picking up items and spreading the neighborhood gossip.

Basha, my mother's older sister, had gotten married and she came home one day to pick up some of her clothing to take to her new house. While Basha was out of the room, my mother slipped quietly into the bedroom and tried on some of Basha's clothing. She thought she looked so beautiful and mature in her sister's clothes! But when she walked out into the living room to show her sister how wonderful she looked, her sister was so angry that she gave my mom a spanking like she'd never had before! That was the last time she did that. But she always said it was worth it, feeling so special and beautiful in her sister's dress.

A few years later my mother went downtown to pick up a few things and told her mother she'd be back within an hour. She dressed up, fixed her hair, and even though she was only 14, she felt like she was 21. The funny thing is, she didn't really need anything from downtown; she just wanted to get out of the house!

But while she was walking down the street, she noticed some pamphlets lying around, and she picked them up to read them. At that moment, a Polish soldier approached and asked her what she's doing on the street spreading Communist propaganda! She was stunned and said she was just looking at them, but he didn't believe her, and he took her to the local jail. Someone went and told her mother where she was, but her mother wasn't able to leave the young children alone, so my mom had to spend the night in the jail. It was a night she would never forget, not even 70 years later, when she first told me the story.

Not long after that, her mother asked her to take her younger brother and sister with her to a neighboring village to buy groceries. My mother couldn't understand it. Why go that far just for potatoes, milk, and flour? Why not shop in the town? And why take the younger siblings? They would only slow her down. But her mother insisted.

So they hiked three miles to the next town, and they were gone for two or three hours. When they came home, the house was empty. Everyone was gone. I can only imagine the fear and anxiety my mother felt as she looked for them. One of their few remaining neighbors told her that the Nazis had come and taken everyone away. I'm sure my mother wondered what had become of Sarah, who could not get out of bed.

But the three of them hunkered down in the house, waiting to see what would happen next.

The next day, loud sirens and German voices over loudspeakers told them to come outside, so she walked out, her little brother and sister on each side of her, holding her hands tightly. The soldiers were pulling people in every direction, and while she managed to keep track of her little sister, she lost her brother, Mendel. People were crying, shouting out for one another. There were gunshots.

I stand there with my family in the streets of Czestochowa, listening to the sounds, smelling the air, imagining what it might have been like when my parents were young, when the Nazis came. I will never forget this moment.

My mother and her sister managed to stay together, although she eventually heard that the Nazis, when they saw how old her mother was and that her sister couldn't walk, shot them both in the house. How she wept.

Eventually, the two of them ended up in Bergen-Belsen for several months and were later transferred to Dachau. Yet they managed to survive.

My mother was a survivor.

~ ~ ~ ~ ~

From there, we go to the Czestochowa ghetto and cemetery, important stops for us. We go into a building that holds birth, marriage, and death records, and I spend a few hours researching my mother and father and their families. We realize that our roots in Poland go back many generations, and we find gravesites for family who we never even knew existed. We walk through the rows of headstones, and I take photos of things that feel important to me.

It was in that ghetto that my uncle Mendel died, only 14 years old, part of a group of teenage resisters machine-gunned down as they tried to flee the ghetto.

That night, after an emotional day, we drive back north, returning to Warsaw, planning on visiting the concentration camp Treblinka the following morning, where all of my family was killed.

When we arrive, much of it reminds me of the other camps we've visited, with the photos and memorabilia that has been collected. I stare closely into every photo, trying to recognize my father or his brother, but so many of those starved faces look the same. But I knew that if I saw my father, I would know. I would recognize him, with his beautiful gray eyes and ears that stuck out a bit.

I have read books about how horrific this concentration camp was, with its many gas chambers and tortured prisoners. I will always wonder how my father and his one brother didn't end up here with the rest of the family. What kept them from dying in Treblinka like everyone else they knew and loved? Maybe they were away the day the soldiers came. Maybe they were taken to a different ghetto.

I close my eyes inside that concentration camp and feel the presence of my family, everyone who suffered there, everyone who was killed there. We stand close and say a prayer in their memory.

That evening, we get on a plane and fly home.

All of this is my imagination, but, God willing, I will go there in 2021.

AFTERWORD

When you start writing a book about your life, it feels like you're sitting in therapy. Writing my first book took approximately seven years. I would start writing and then put it on the shelf for six months, then pick it up again and get back to work on it. It was painful and soul-searching, and it took me some time to work up the nerve to actually finish it.

It came out the year that I lost my mother. So much has happened since then, and I felt strongly about sharing the rest of my life with all of you. I've received so many great comments, testimonies, and prayer requests since my first book came out. I've been asked advice. And with this book, it feels like everything has come full circle.

Who knows? Perhaps there's another book in my future, if I'm blessed enough to live that long. Whatever the case might be, I'm grateful for every experience I've had and thankful for the millions of people I've gotten to meet along the way. I'm amazed at all the opportunities we've had, and so blessed to have a family made up of people who are literally my best friends.

We are certainly living in unsettled times.

I feel a deep burning in my soul to tell my story everywhere I go, because I know that we will not prevent disasters like the Holocaust from happening again if we don't know and remember our history.

I have tried to be transparent in everything I've written. I know the only way you can help someone is if you've lived what they're going through yourself. My prayer is that the stories of my life will help you get through a loss, a divorce, depression, anxiety, loneliness, and fear. Obviously, I've felt, or been through, all of those things.

But I also have to say that God is faithful and true. Remember that when you are in the middle of it.

I'll end this book with the chorus from a song my daughters have written:

This is not my battle,
This is not my war.
I don't have to worry
Or fight it anymore.
You have gone before me
And I will sing your song.
Trusting in the victory
That you've already won.
It's yours, Lord

Amen.

ACKNOWLEDGMENTS

Thank You God, for Your blessings. Thank You, Messiah, Yeshua, Savior, Redeemer, Counselor, Provider, Healer, and Friend. The great I Am!

Thank You for the life You have allowed me to live. Thank You for having my back when I couldn't see the future. Thank You for Your mighty shield. Thank You for being my confidante when I felt alone and there was no one else to talk to. Thank You for opportunities I never dreamed of. Thank You for letting me take refuge under Your wings. Thank You for going before me to fight every battle on my behalf. Only with Your covering have I survived.

Thanks to my beautiful family who is my life: my children and their spouses, who are talented, hard-working, and loving; and, to my grandchildren, whom I adore.

Thank you to all of our dear friends and fans who have stood beside us and supported our ministry. You know who you are!

I'm blessed to have crossed paths with all of you.

If you would like to stay up-to-date regarding our planned trip to Poland in 2021, our upcoming trips to Israel, our non-profit (www.fiii.org), and receive word on any new music or projects that we are working on, please follow our website and Facebook page. We will provide stories and photos as they are available!

www.theisaacs.com

from jewish roots, poverty, illness, seclusion, stardom and more....

Meet Lily Isaacs

The Inspirational Legacy & Life Story of Lily Isaacs

A talented daughter of Holocaust survivors, Lily Isaacs is a woman who has felt pain and loss, and found incomparable joy of a life with Jesus Christ. Together, she and her children form the beloved and multi-award winning group The Isaacs. Throughout the pages discover the inspirational legacy of this family's faith journey. Whether struggling with an unknown faith, surviving breast cancer, overcoming heartbreaking moments or a challenging career, Lily's steady refrain has been one of God's constant love, comfort, and strength.

you don't
CRY
out loud
The Lily Isaacs story

Foreword By Andy Andrews New York Times best selling author

New Leaf Press
A Division of New Leaf Publishing Group

978-0-89221-724-3 | $14.99